Really Easy Patterns
Coloring Book

50 easy patterns for beginners to coloring, designed to help you relax, unwind, and get creative with your artwork!

ISBN: 9798390290002

For more information and to stay up to date on new coloring books, visit our website at

www.meghanjamescreations.com

This book belongs to:

_____

Disclaimer:

Before You Get Started

Hi there, darling! Welcome to the **REALLY EASY PATTERNS COLORING BOOK, [VOL. 1].** We're so happy you're here -- you've got **50** pages that are just begging for you to bring them to life with your imagination!

We believe in you and your art! It's our pleasure and privilege to empower you towards maximum creative success, so we've included some fun tools in this book, just for you.

TESTER PAGES

We know it can be super aggravating when you're coloring with non-erasable tools and the color isn't quite what you had hoped. Or even worse, when you can't remember which colored instrument gave you that pigment you just loved! That's why we included the **tester pages** for you. Use these lines and bubbles as a way to try different colors, label them, and make notes for yourself -- before you get started on any of your coloring!

BLEEDER PAGES

It's a real pain when you're coloring one page and your marker/pen/ink decides it wants to color the three pages behind it. The **bleeder pages** in the back of the book are designed to test those sneaky tools that may or may not run through into the pages behind them.

OH NO! MY COLOR RAN THROUGH!

Hey, at least you found out beforehand, right? *We always recommend that you add some scratch paper, plastic, or newspaper behind the design you're working on* to make sure that the design you're bringing to life doesn't accidentally bring other designs to life. It also may be helpful to mark the tool you're using in the tester pages as a tool that will run through the paper.

WHAT IF I NEED A DO-OVER?

One of the most amazing things about art is sometimes, you'd do it over. If you need another copy of the design you're working on, you can always visit our website and purchase standalone pages. No need to buy another copy of the book -- unless you want to!

ABOVE ALL, this is your creative space to do whatever your heart desires. Happy creating!

Tester Page #1

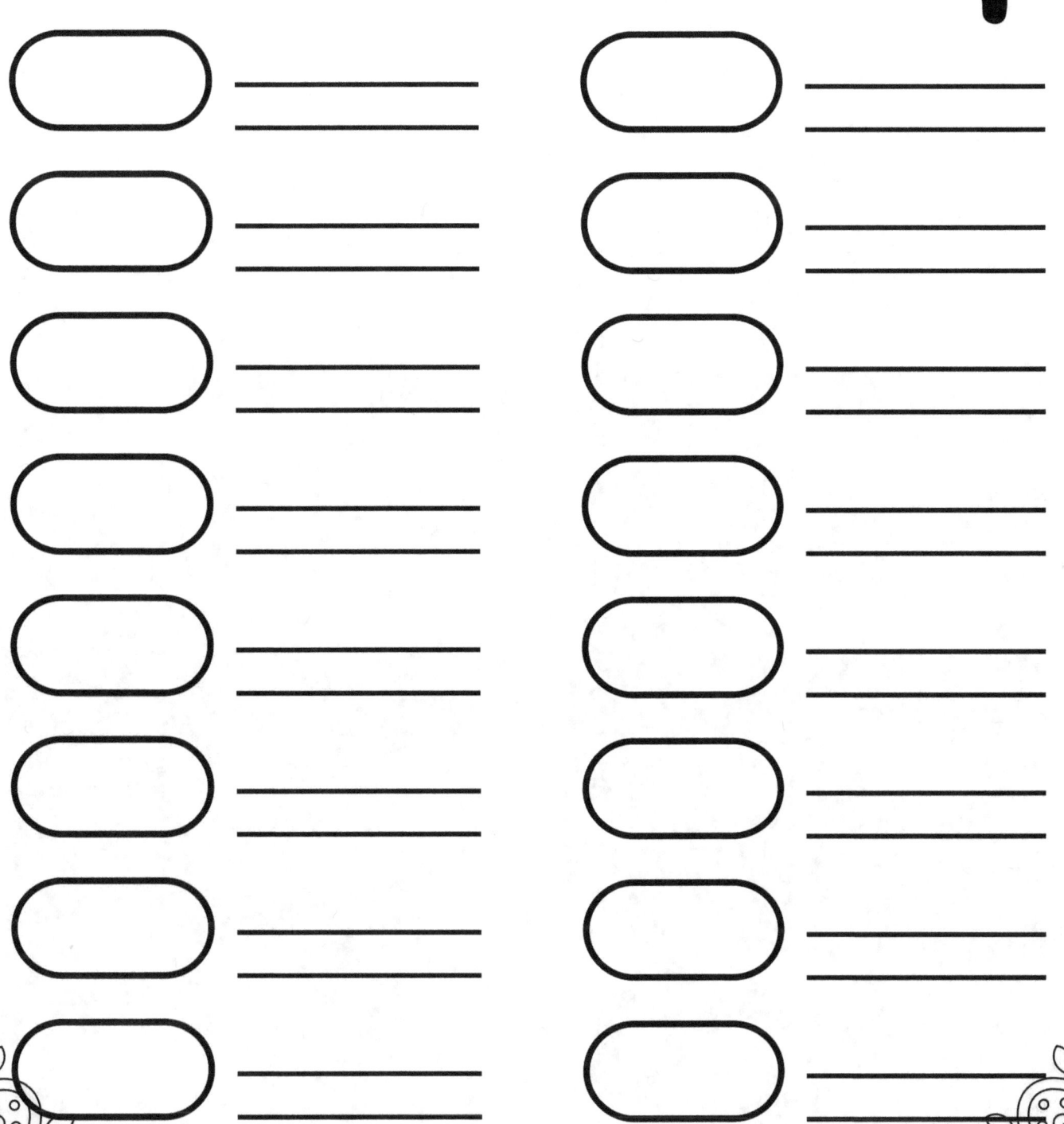

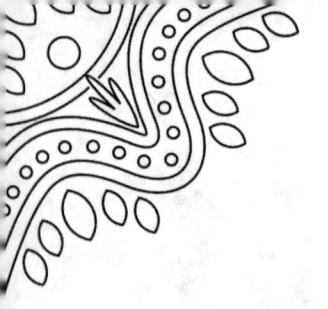
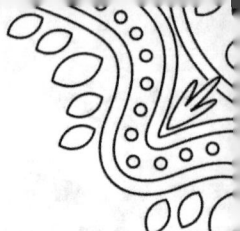
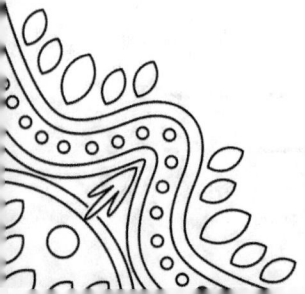
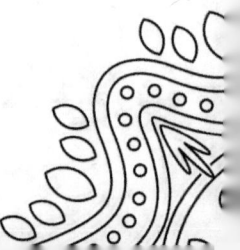

Tester Page #2

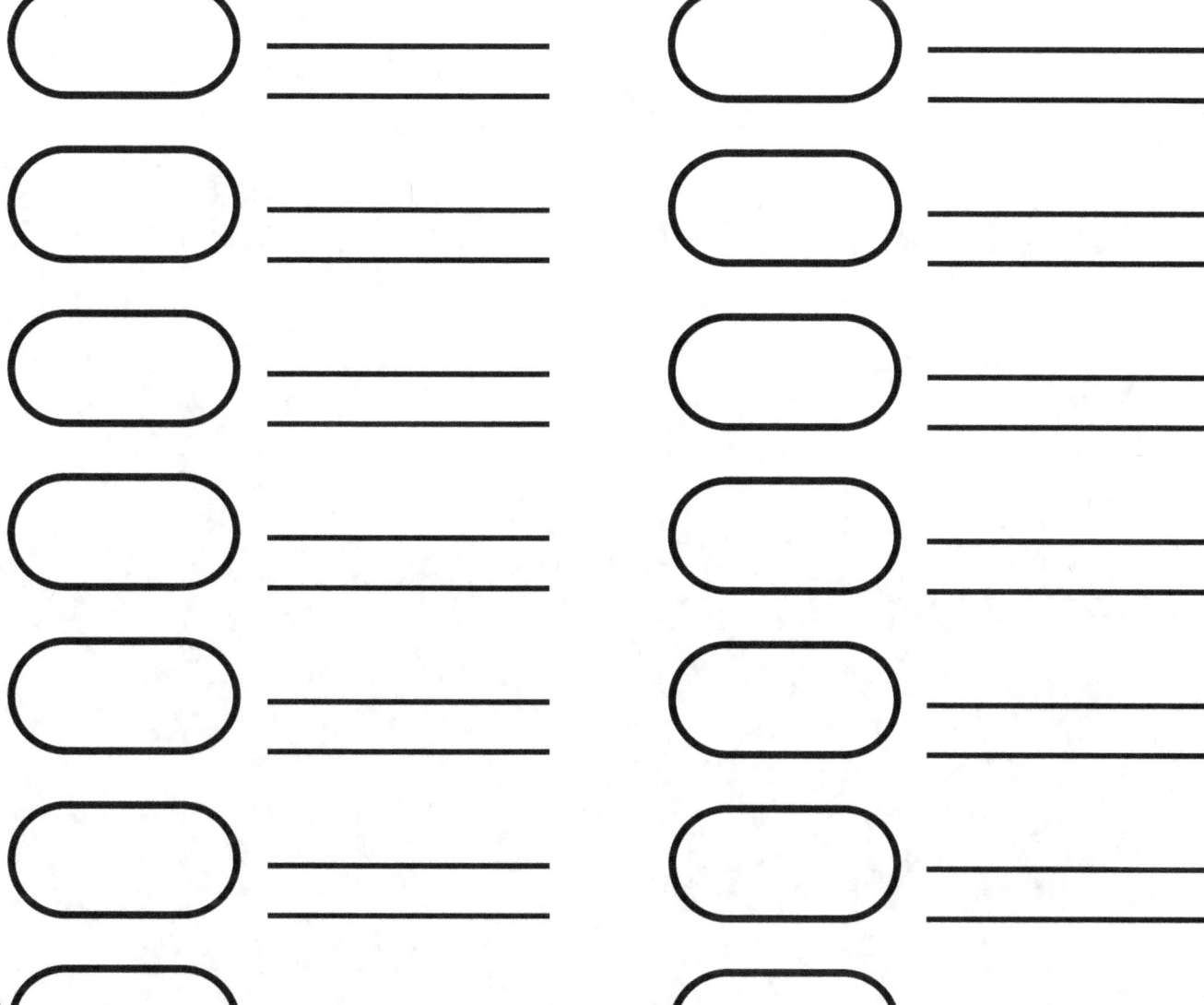

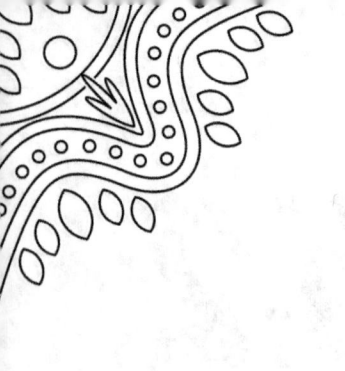
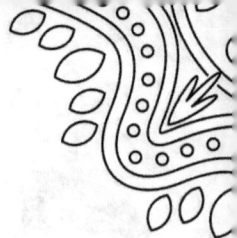
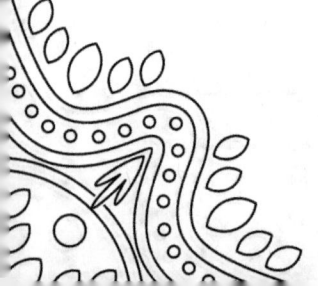
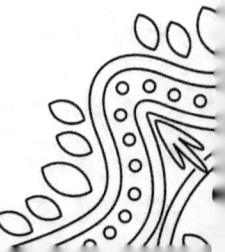

Tester Page #3

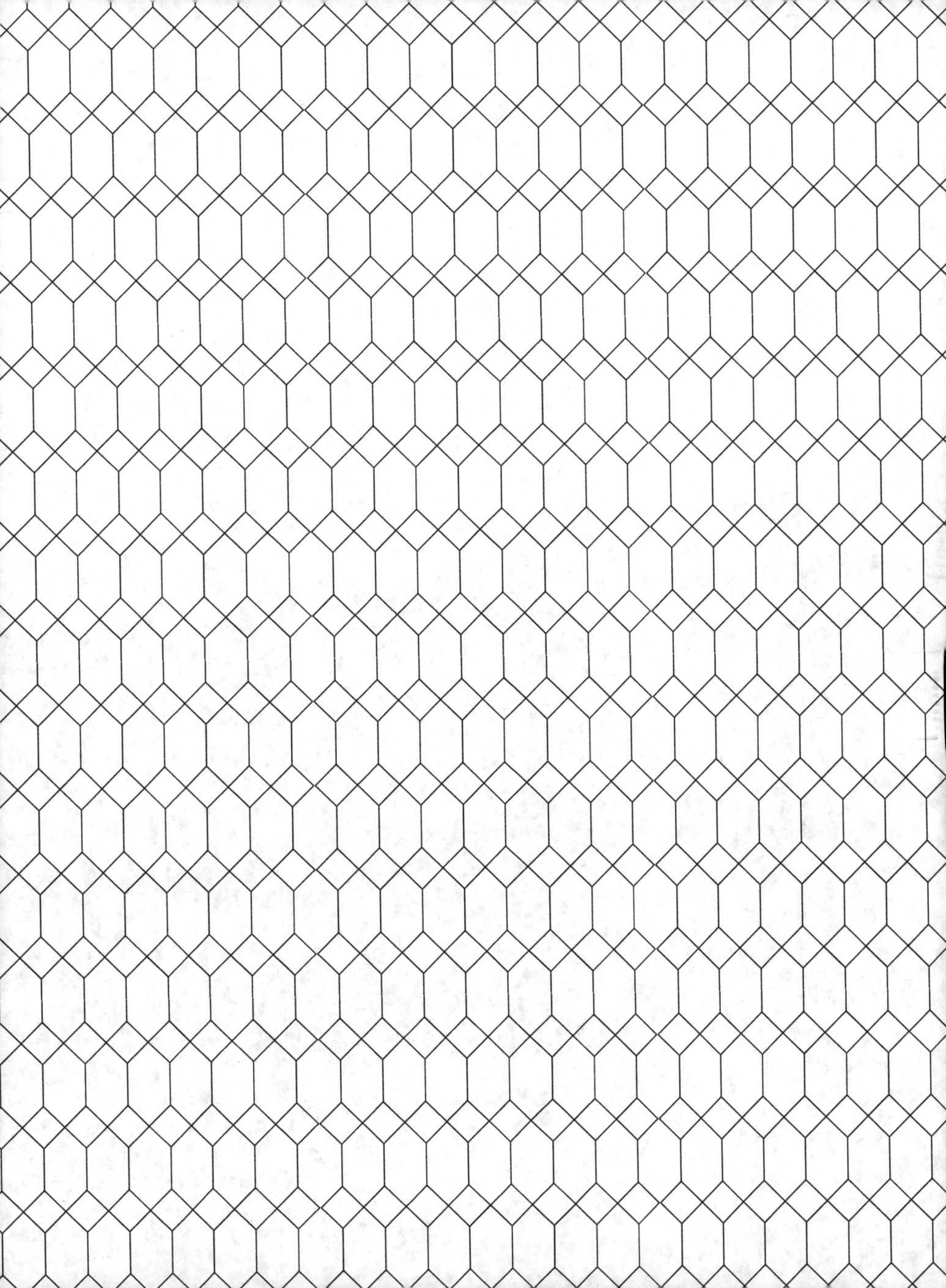

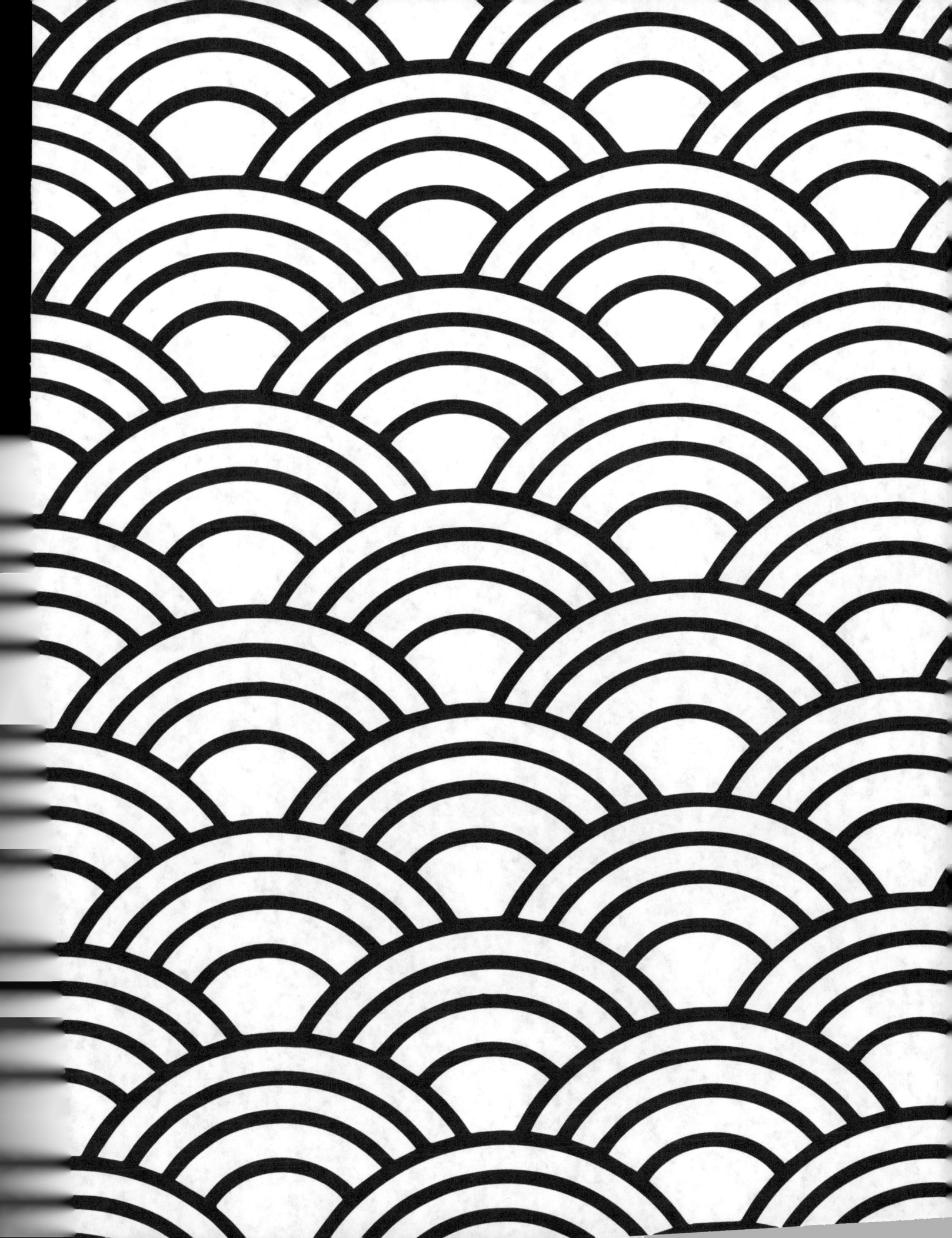

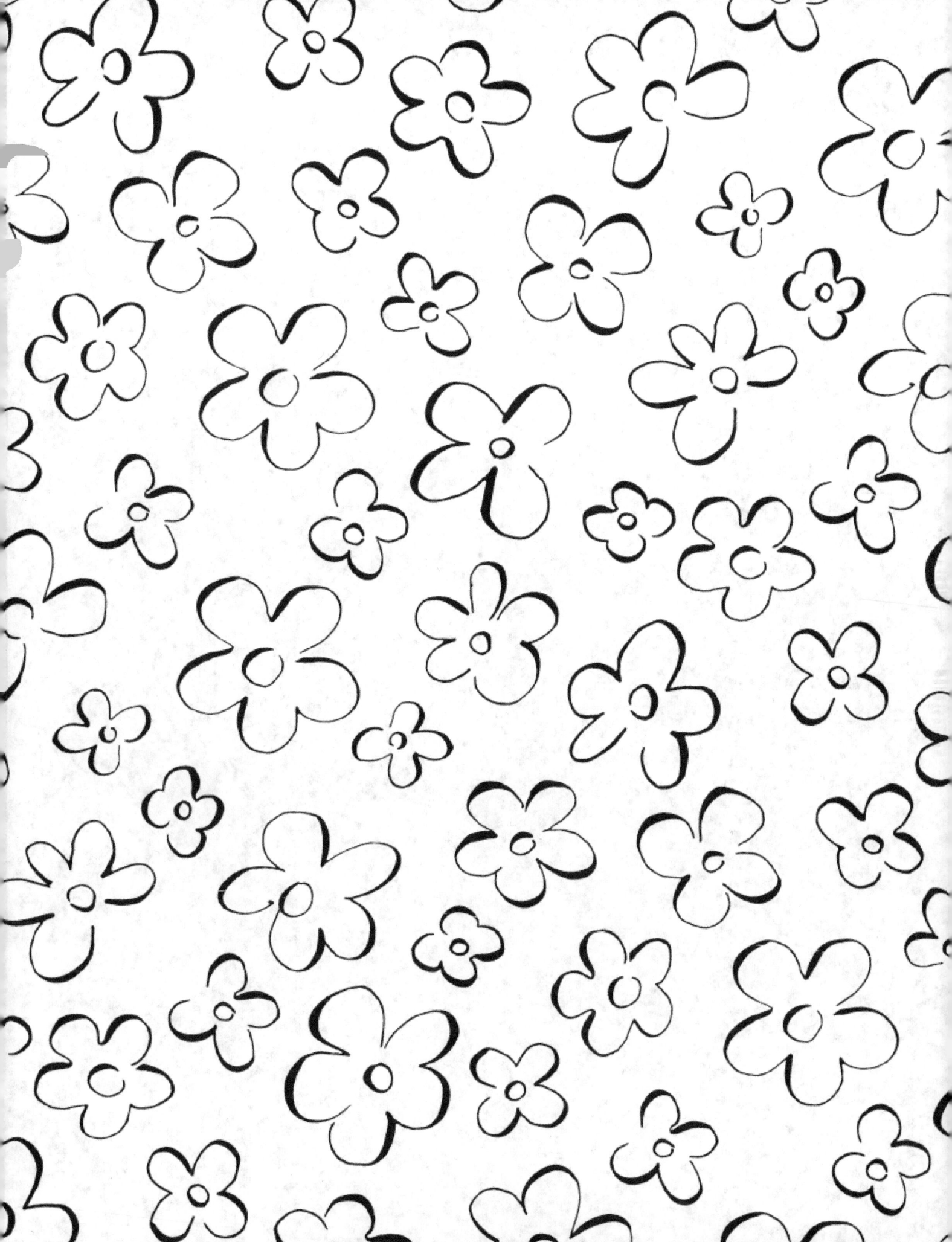

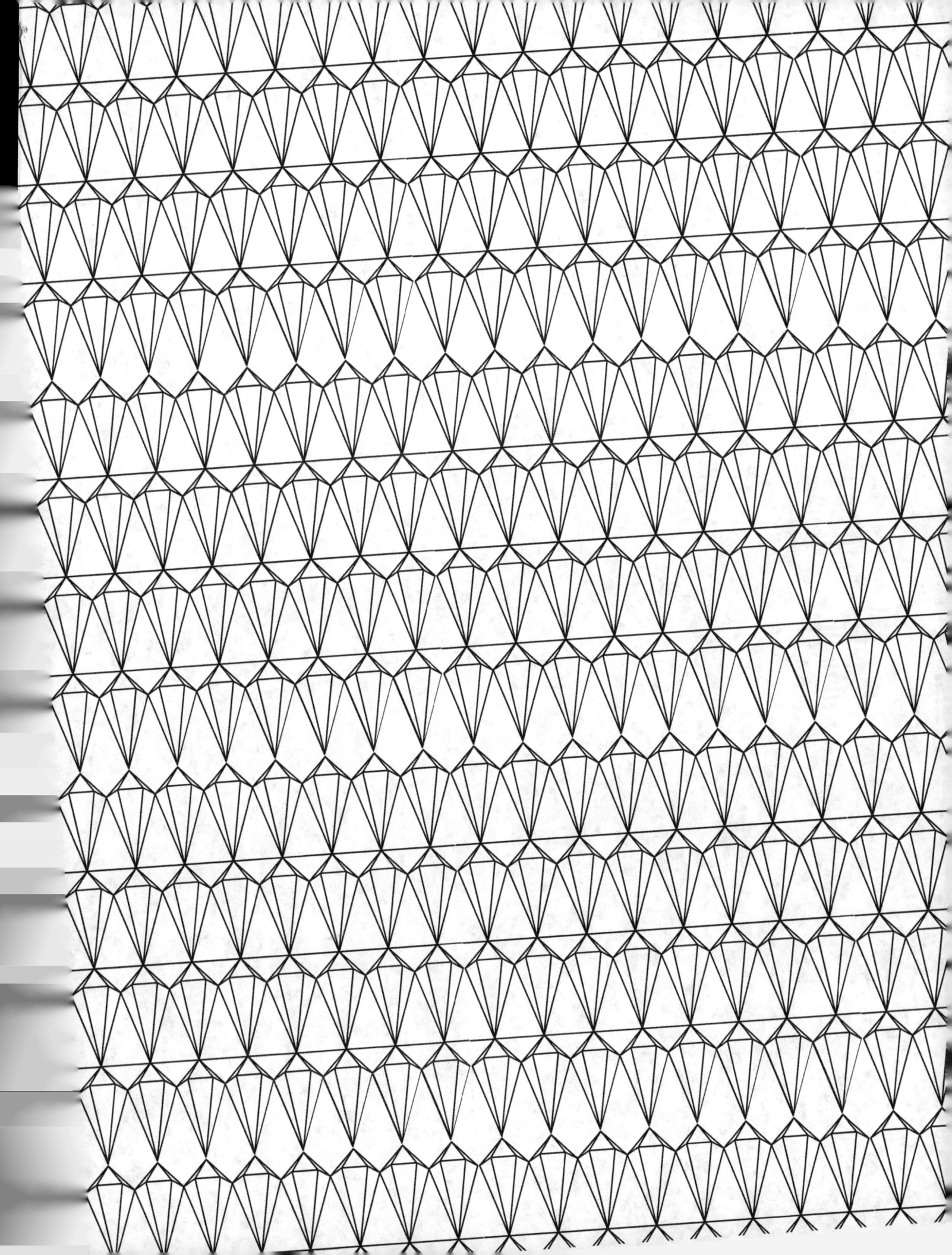

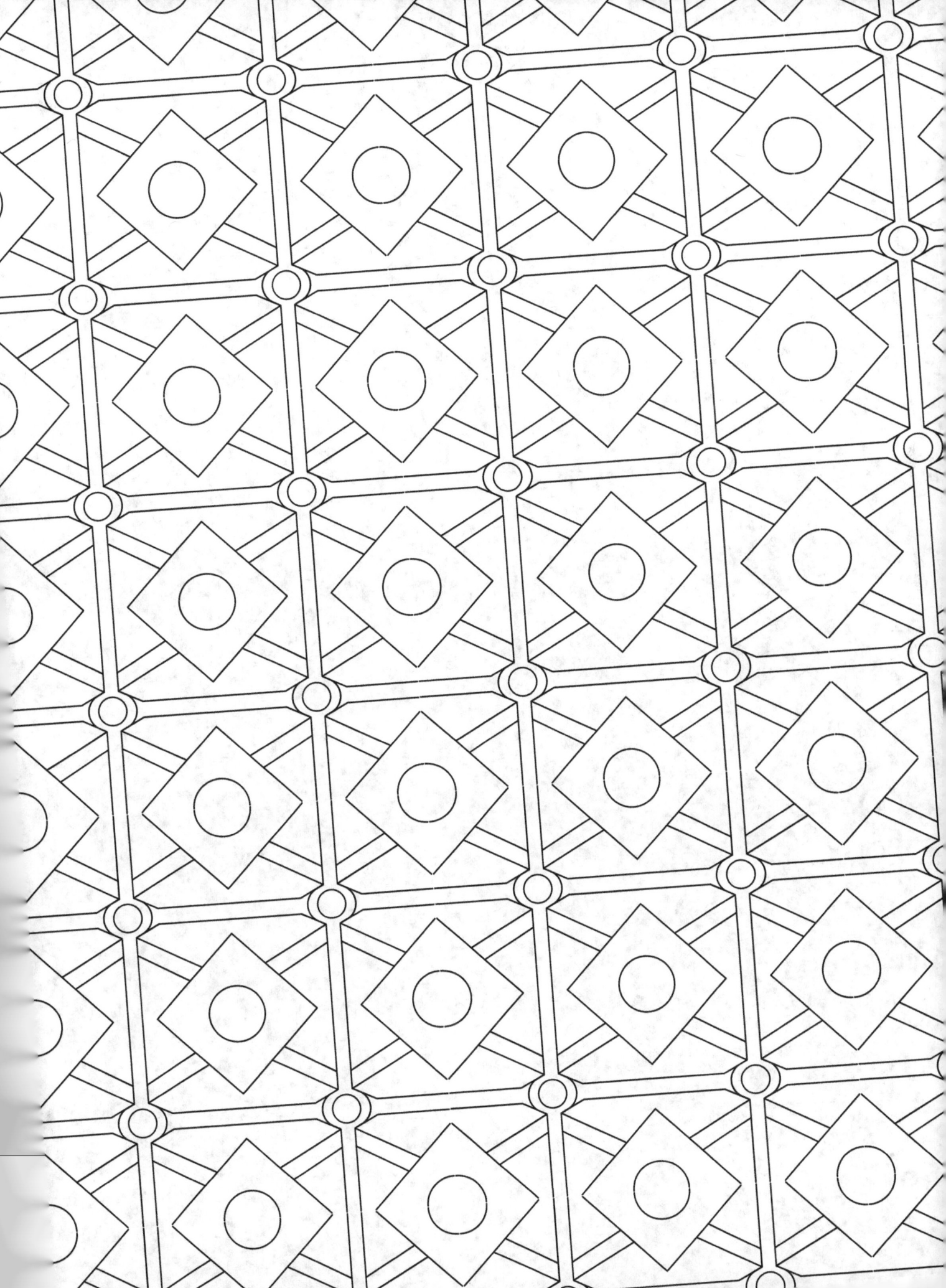

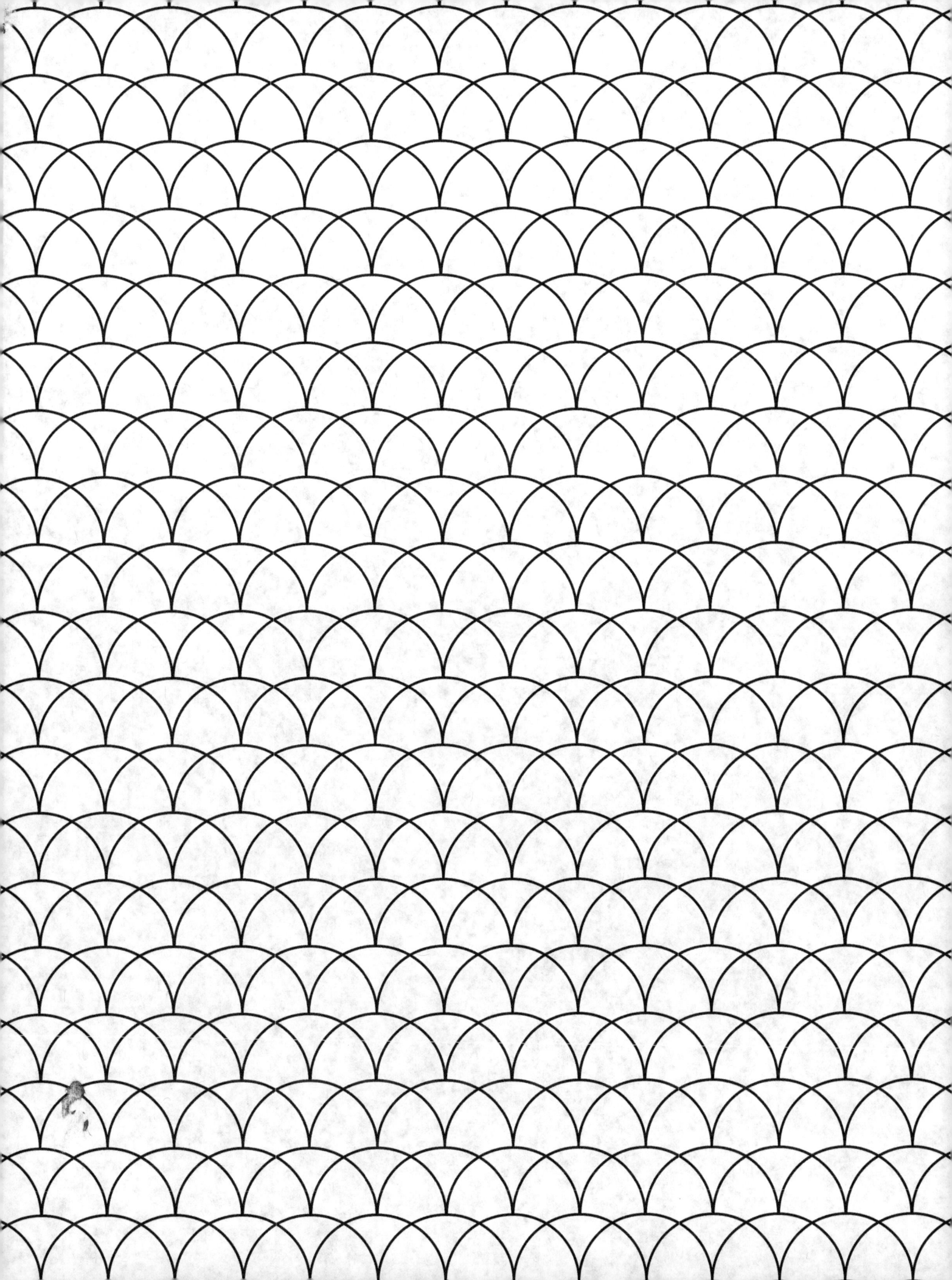

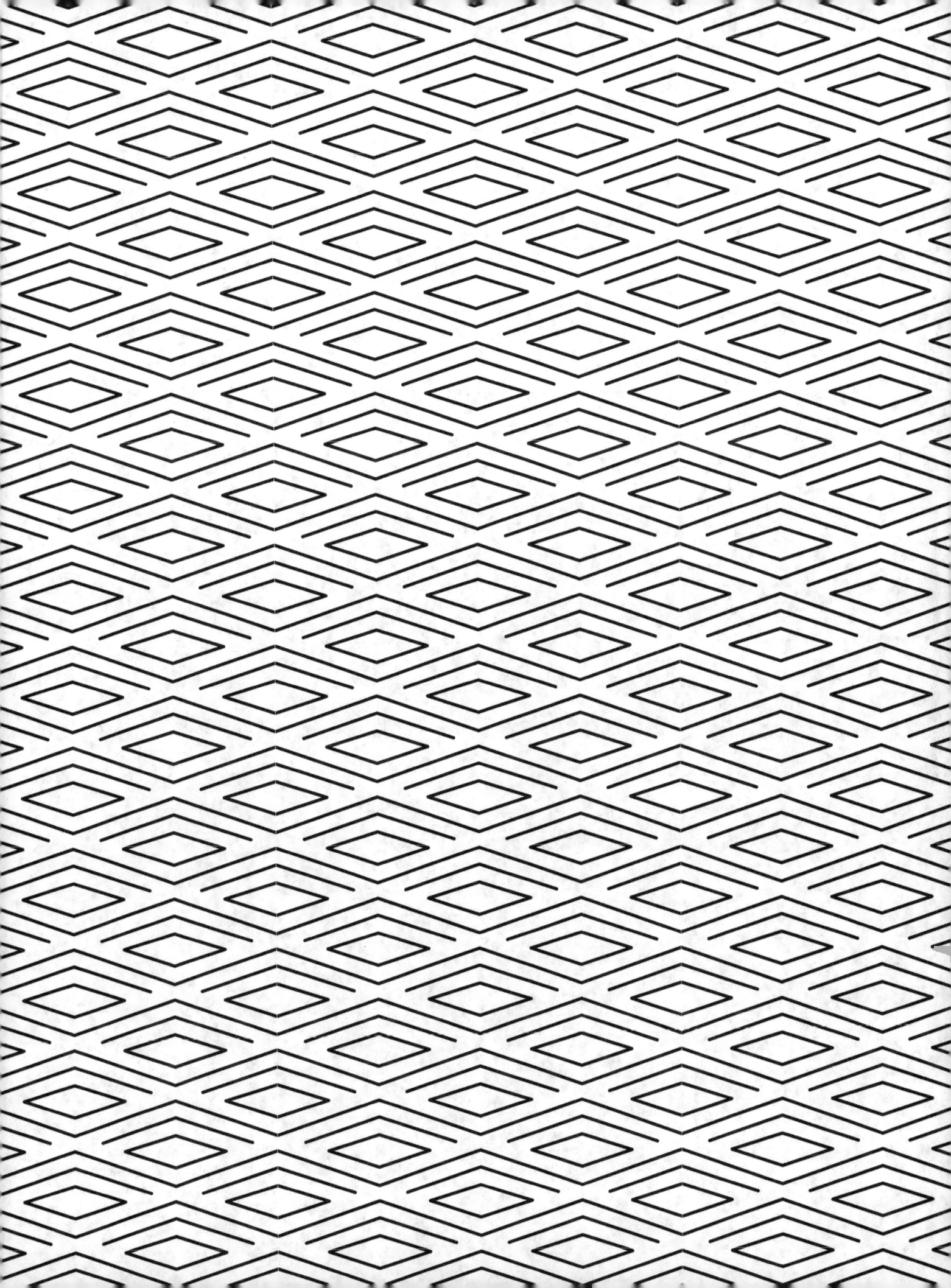

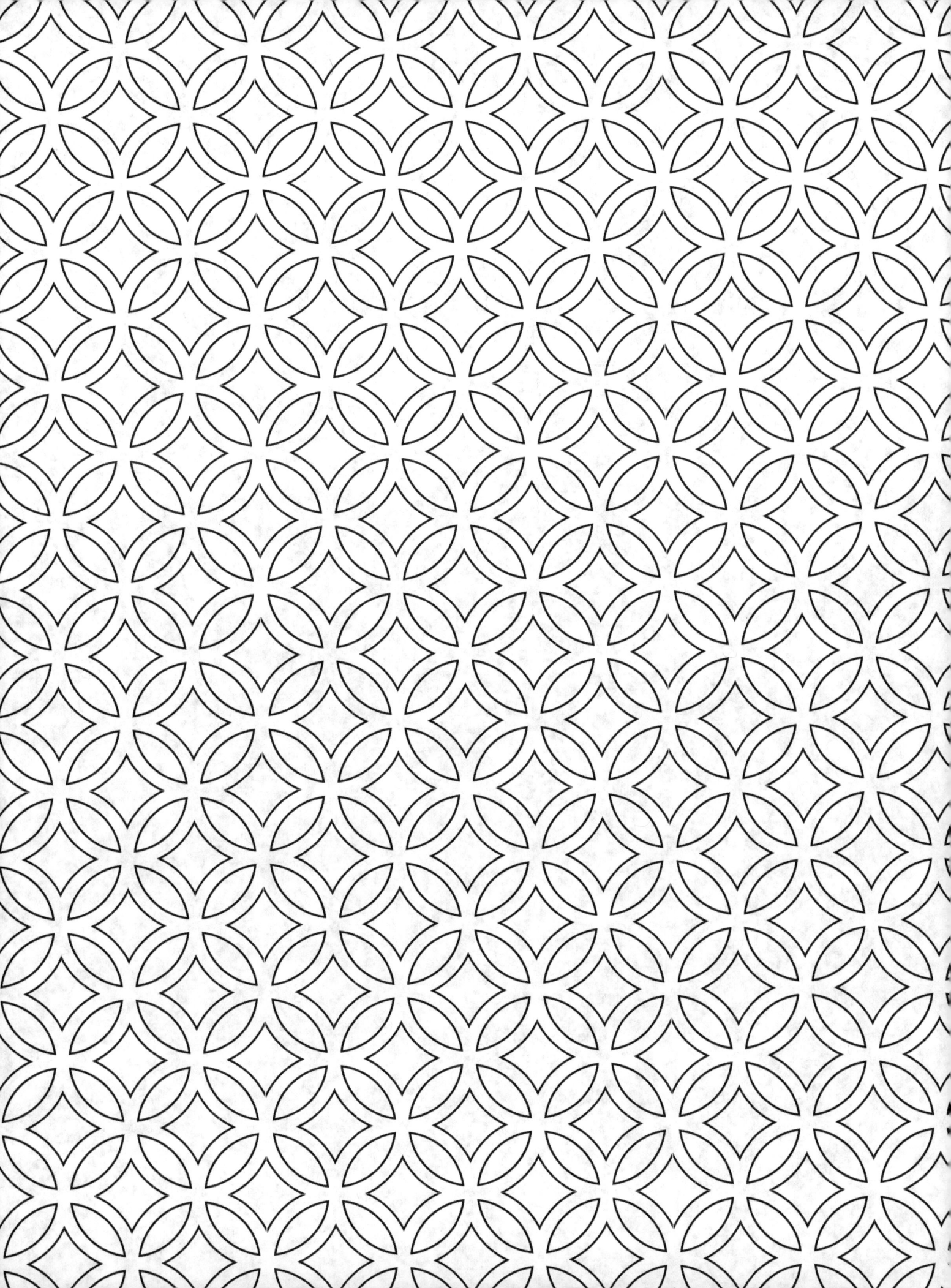

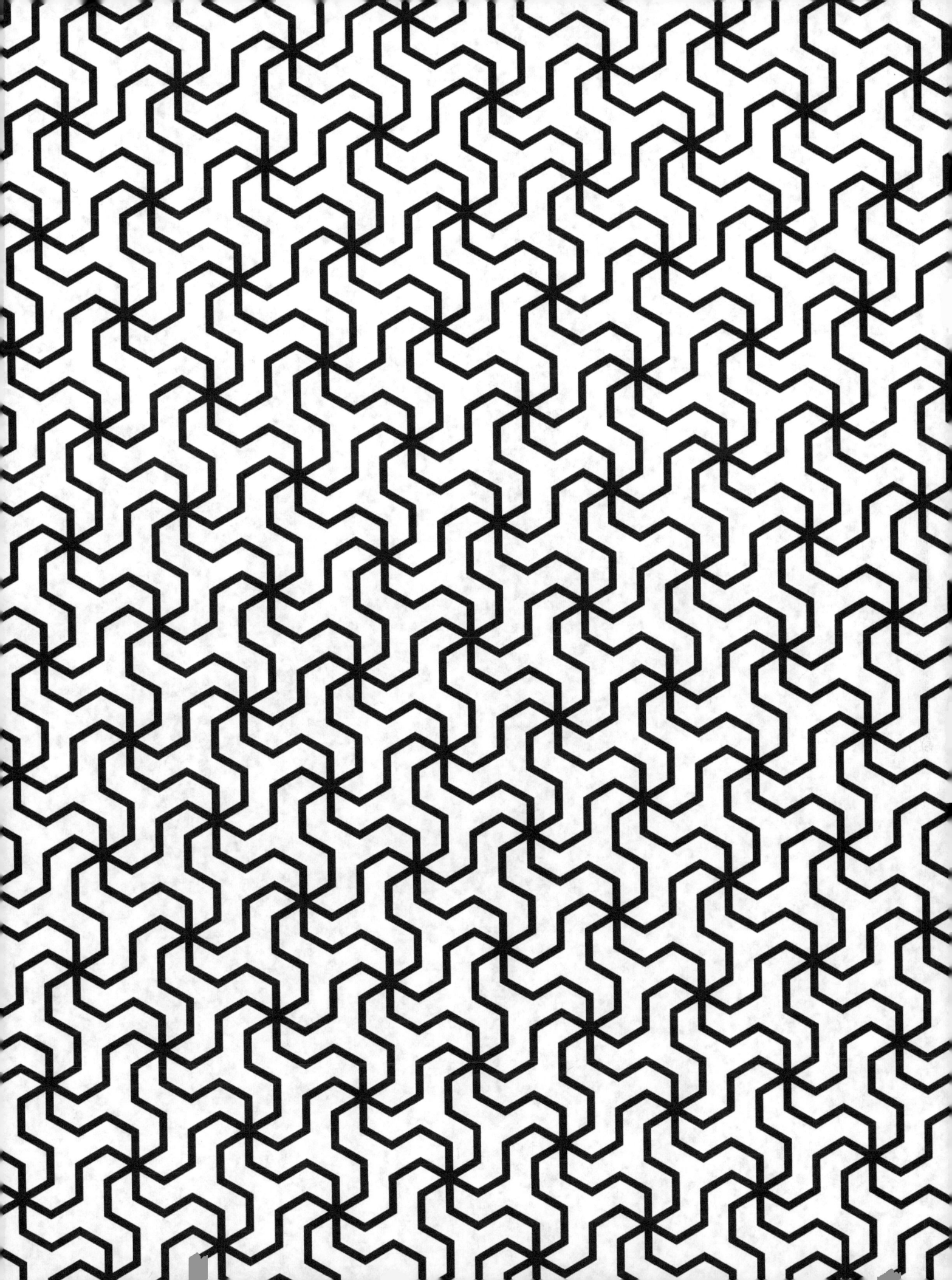

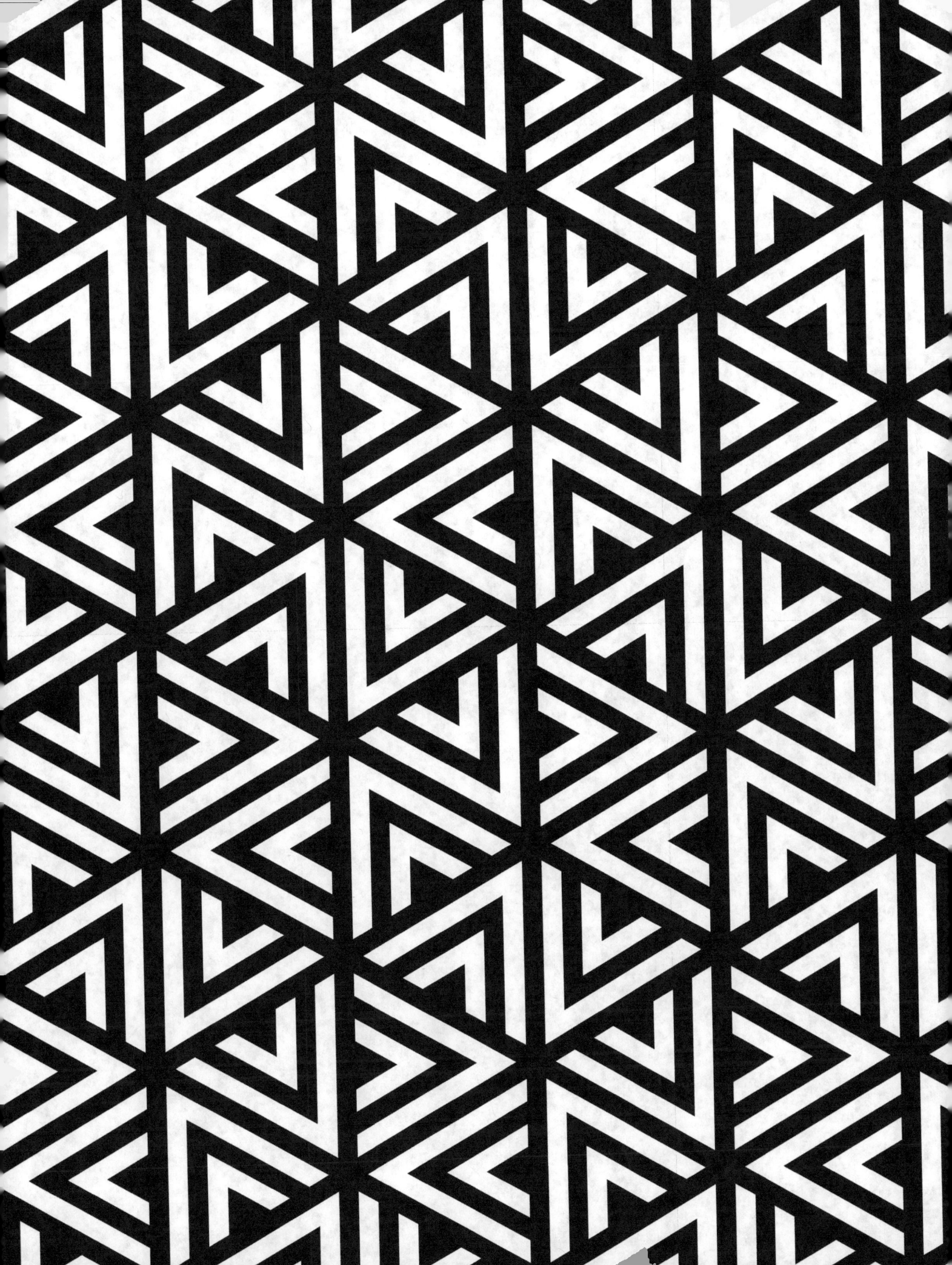

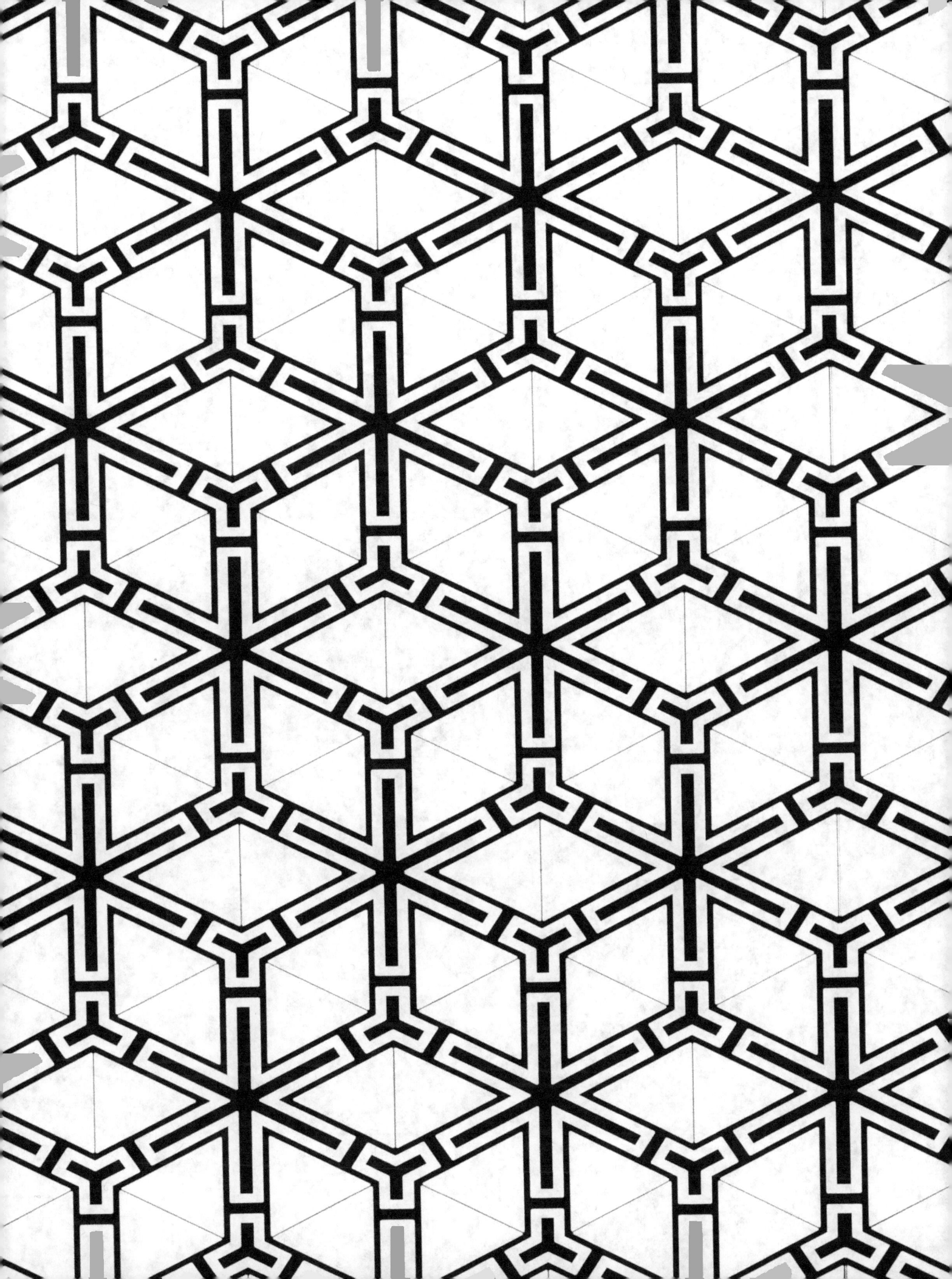

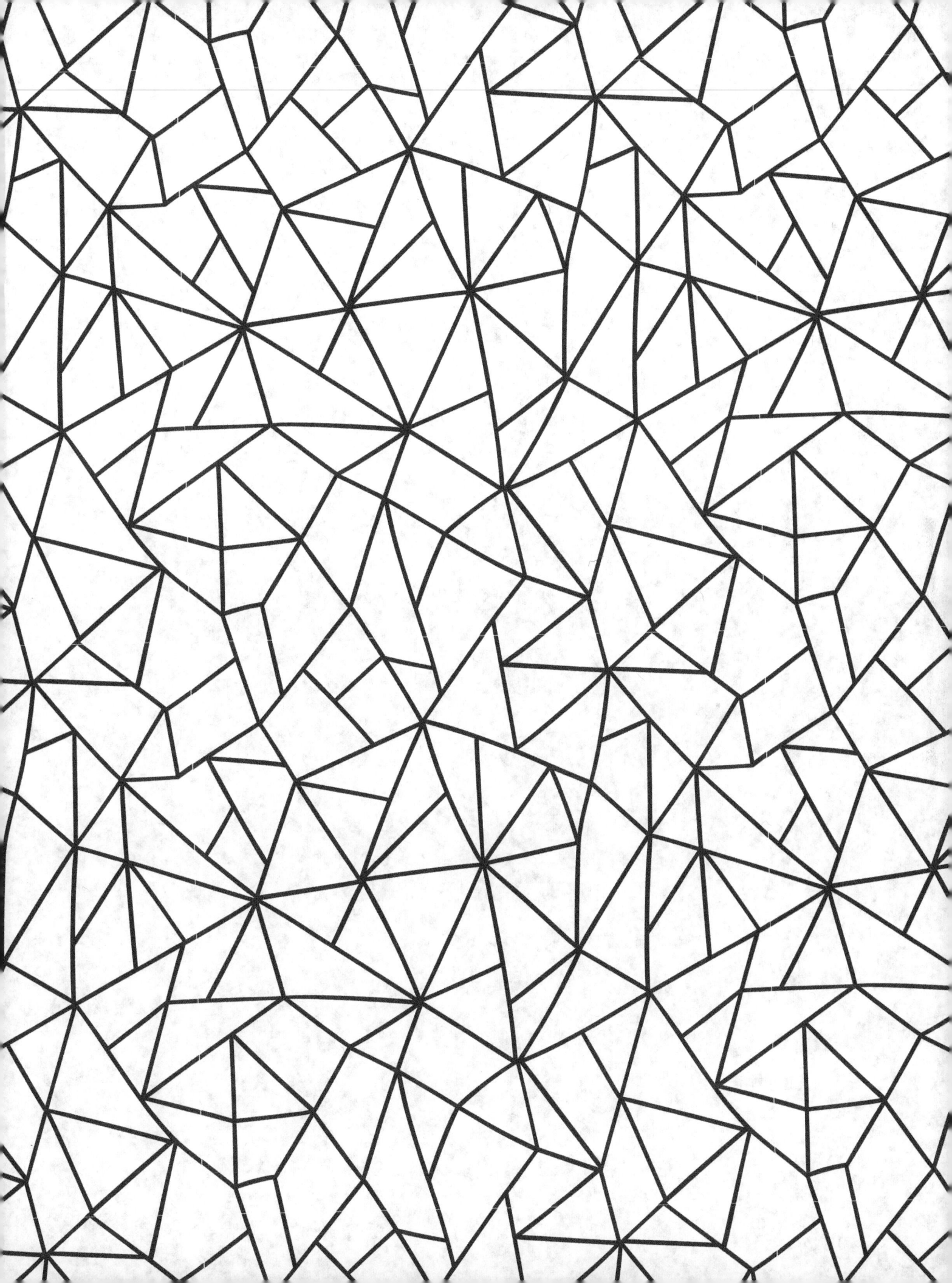

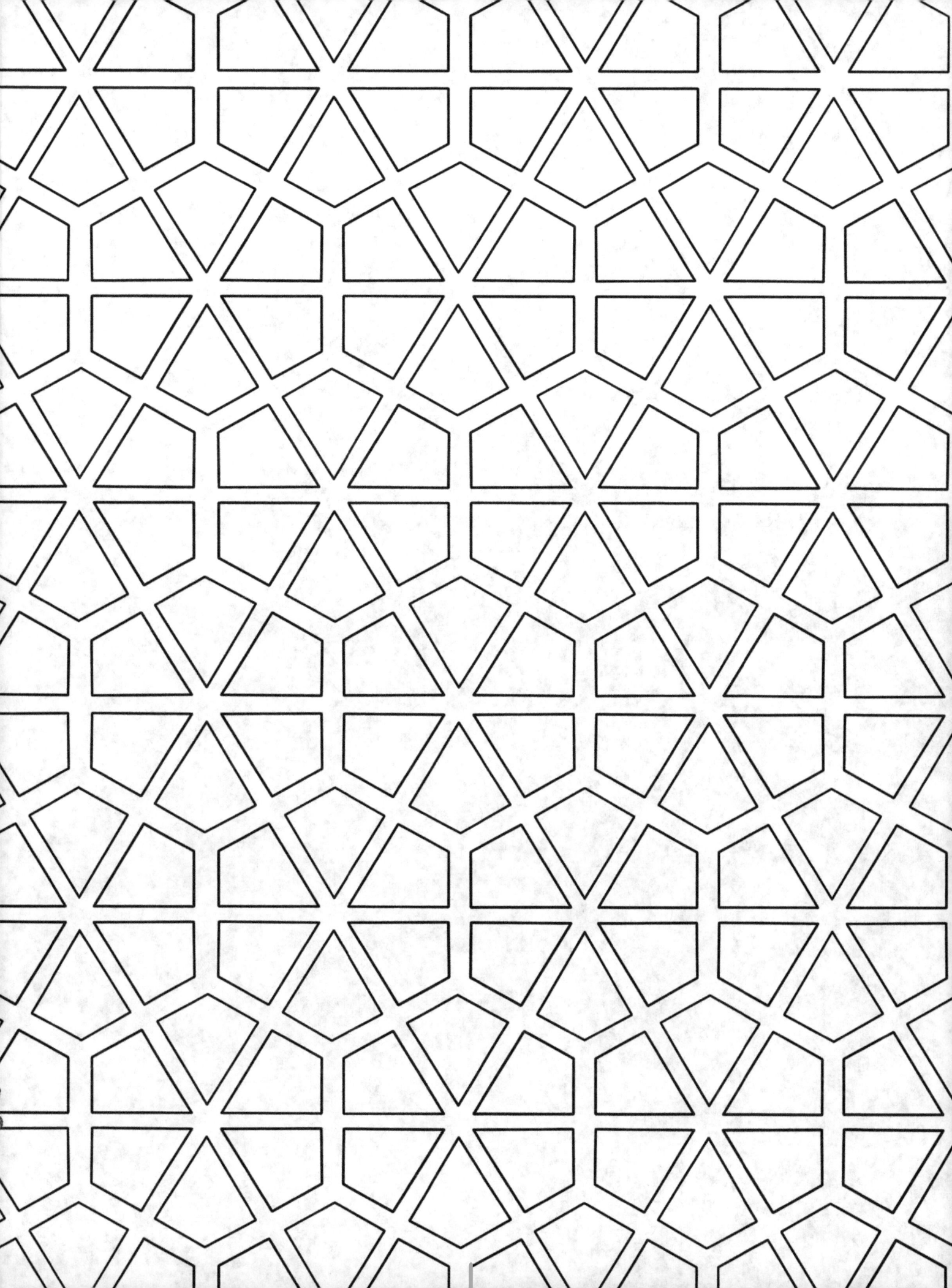

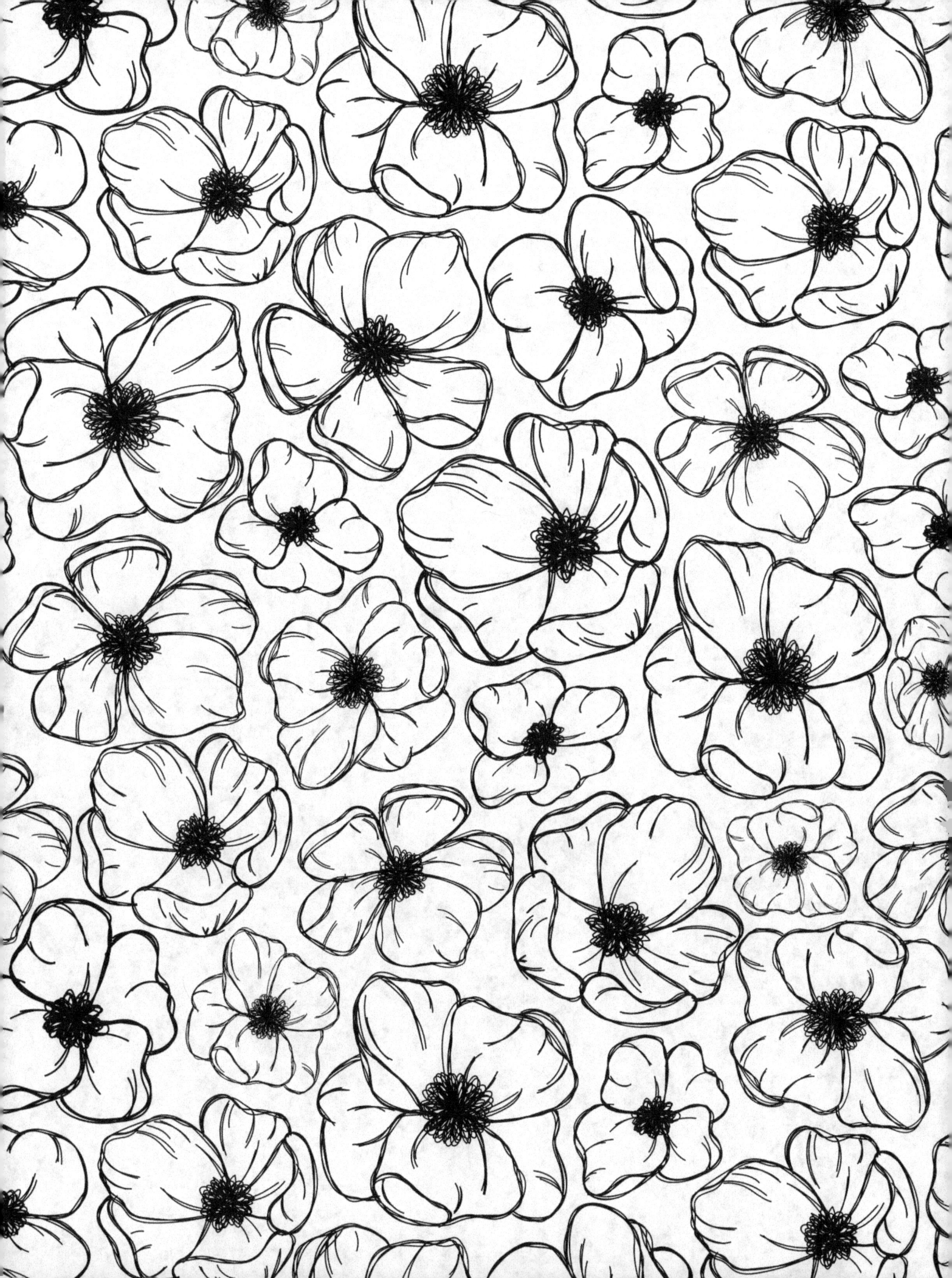

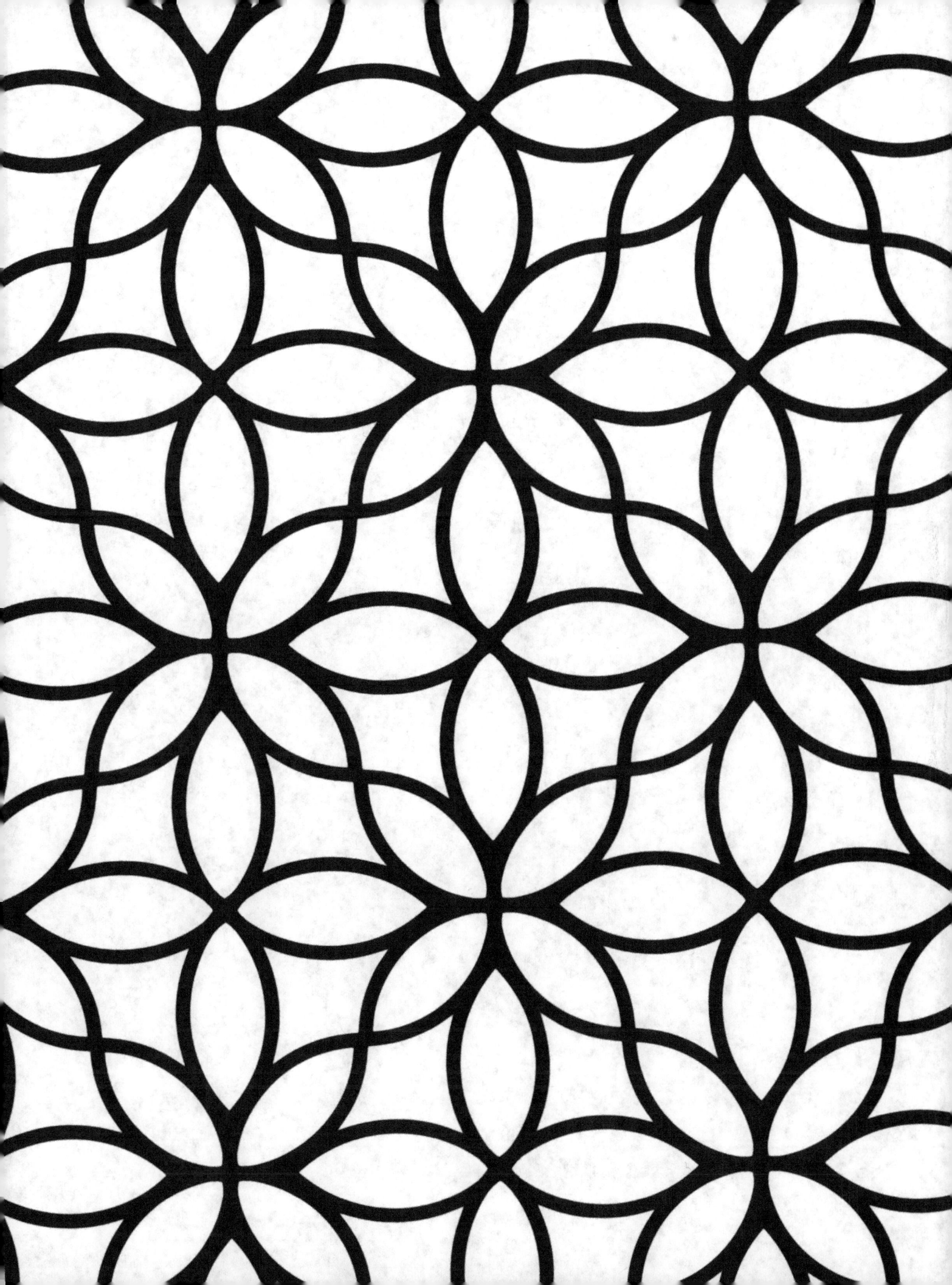

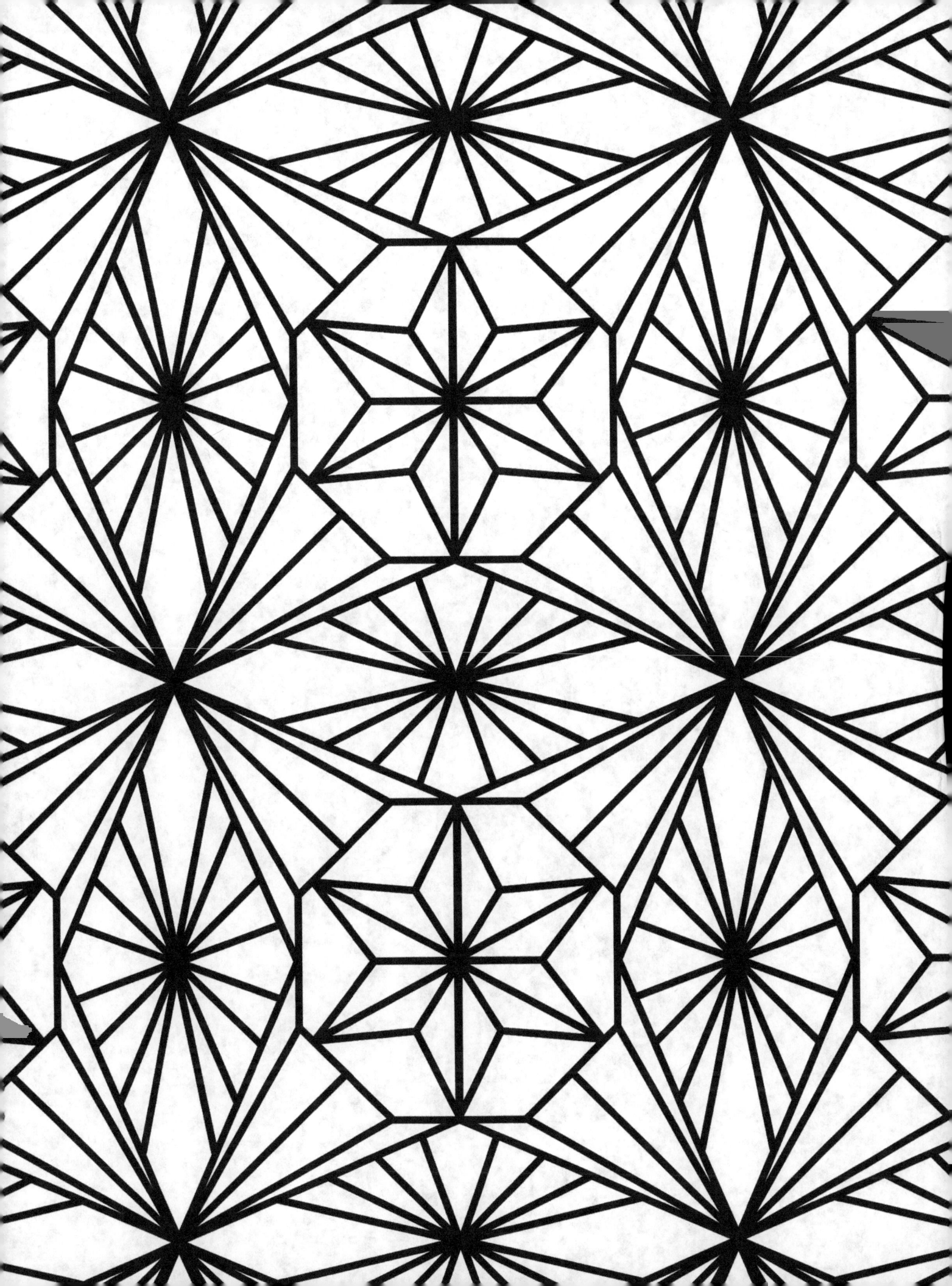

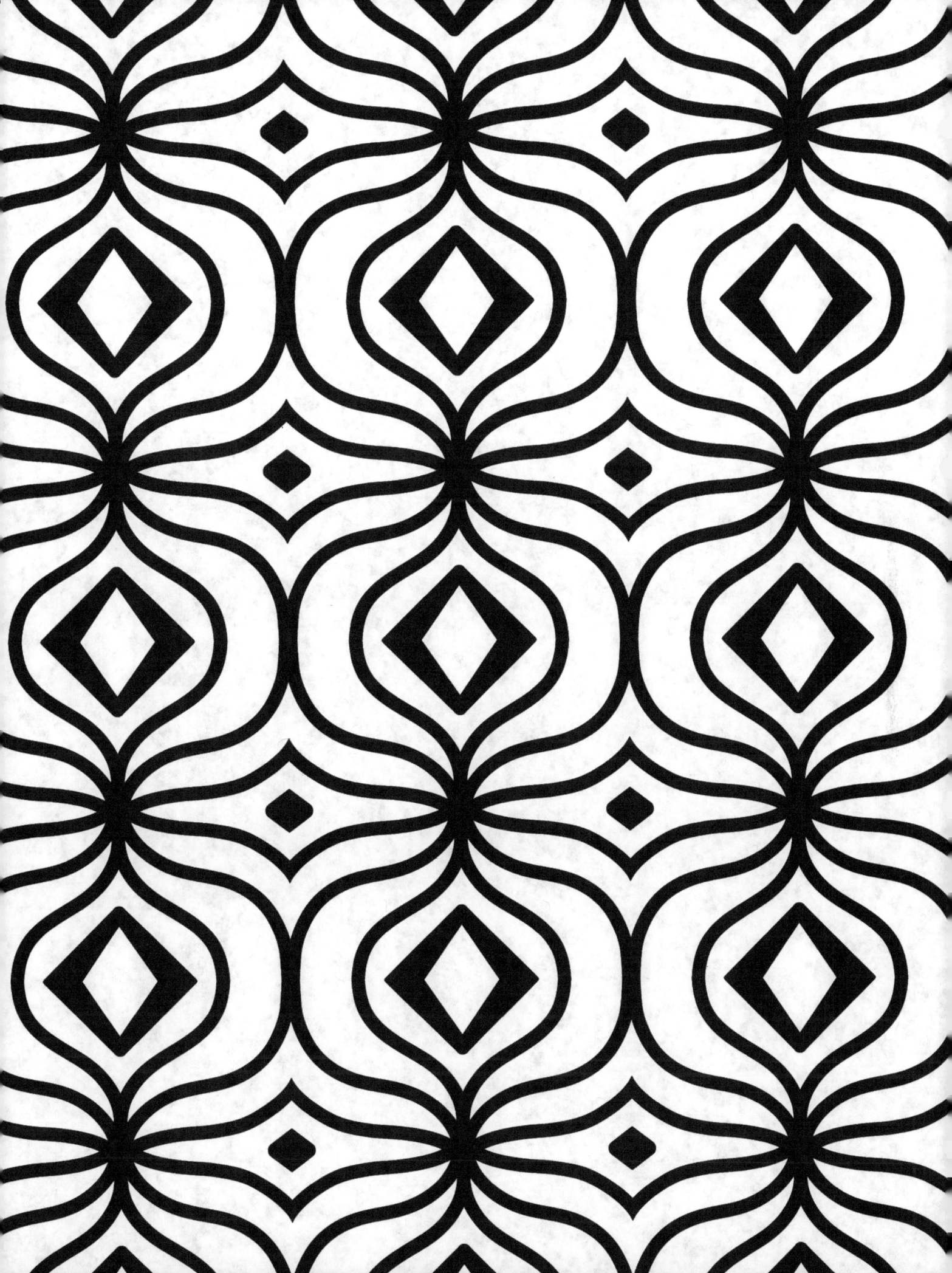

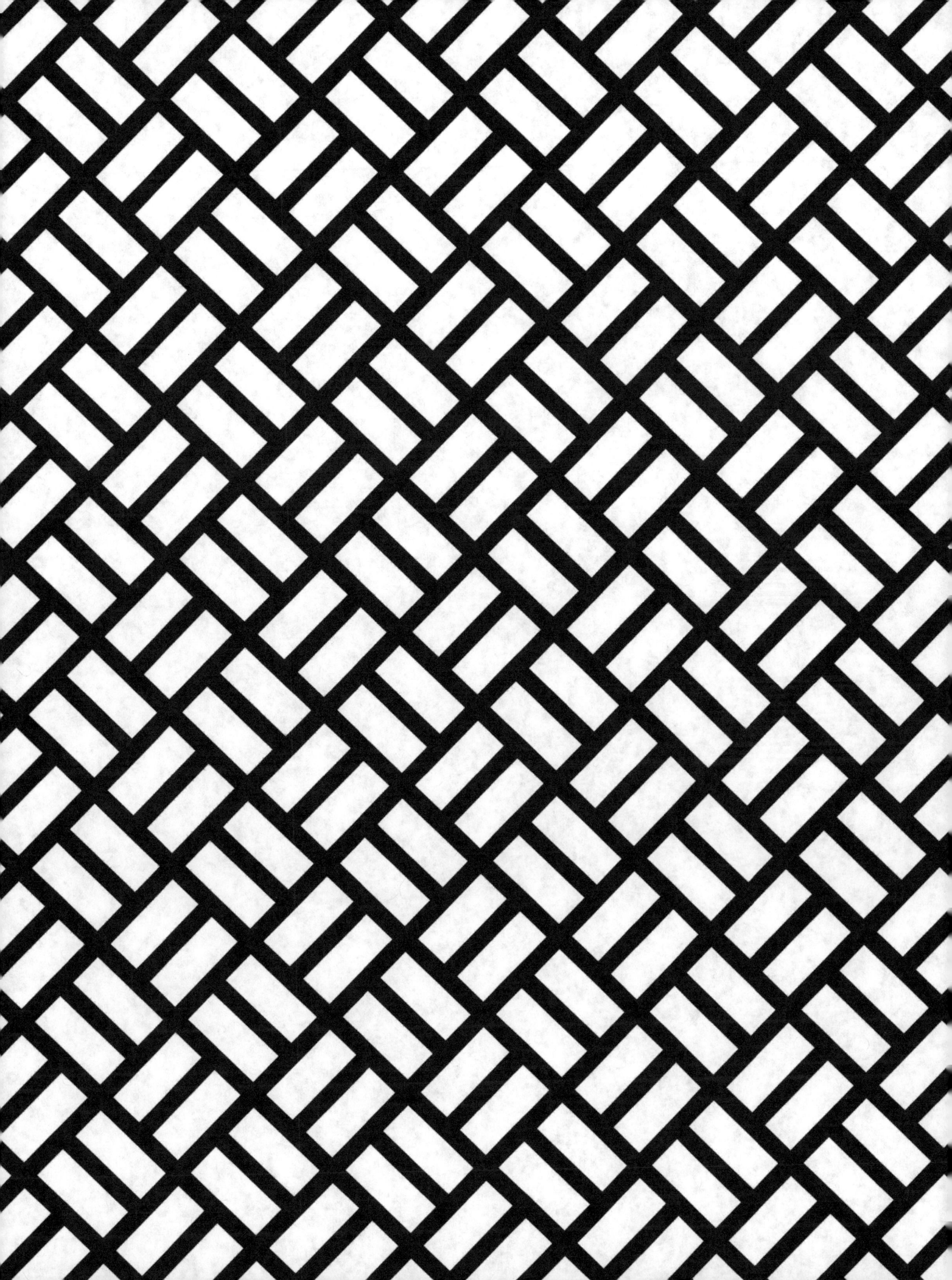

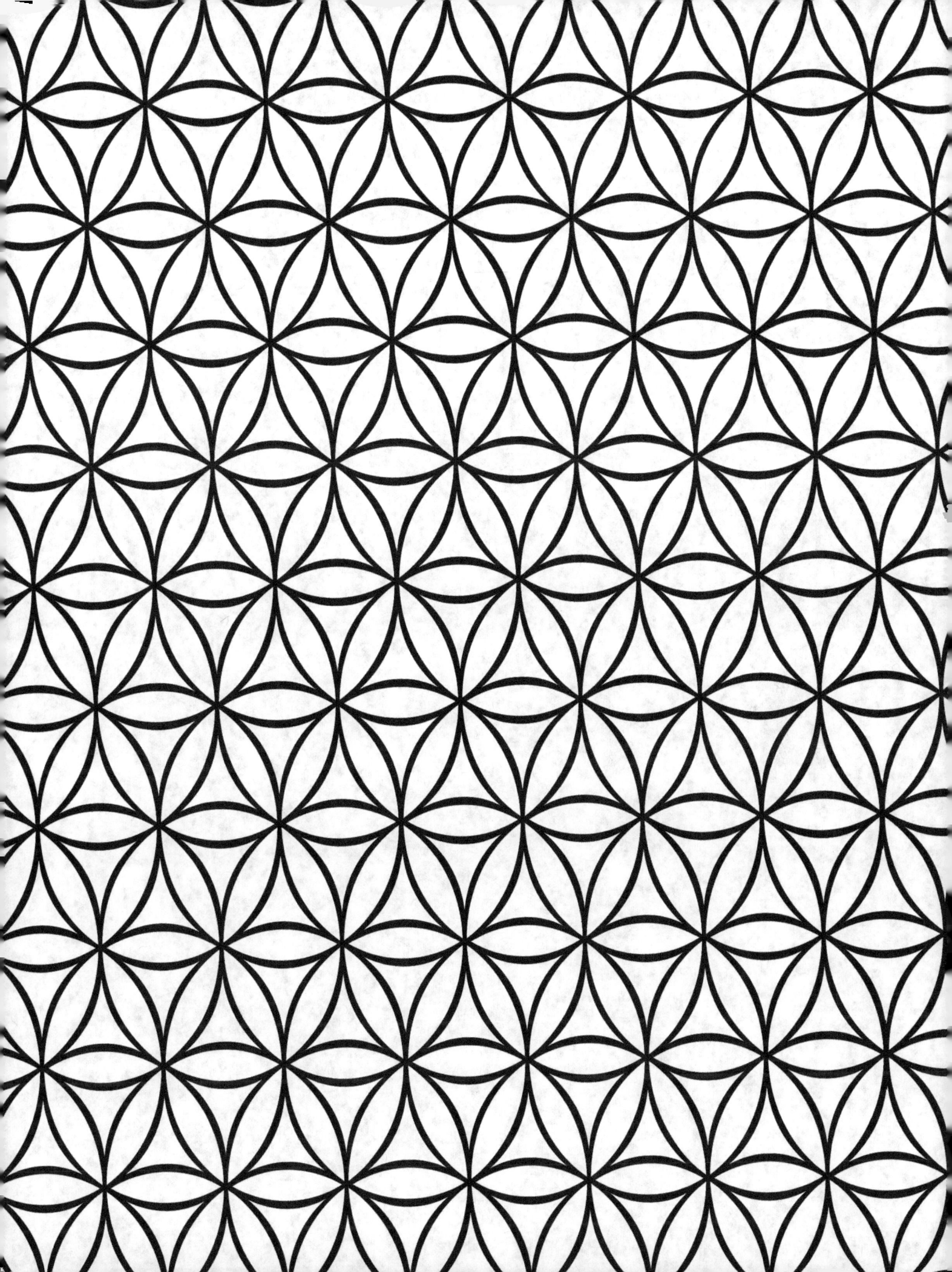

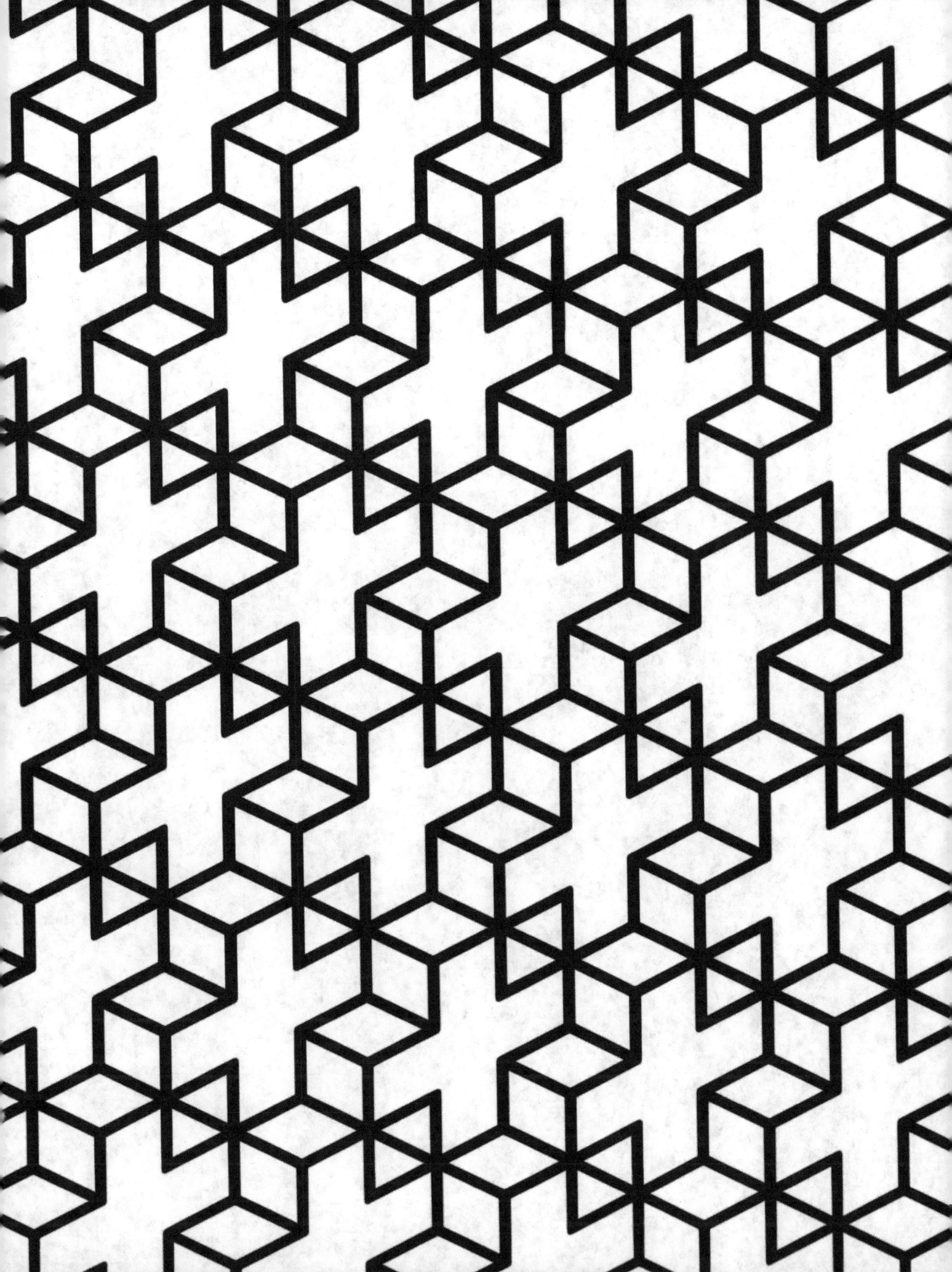

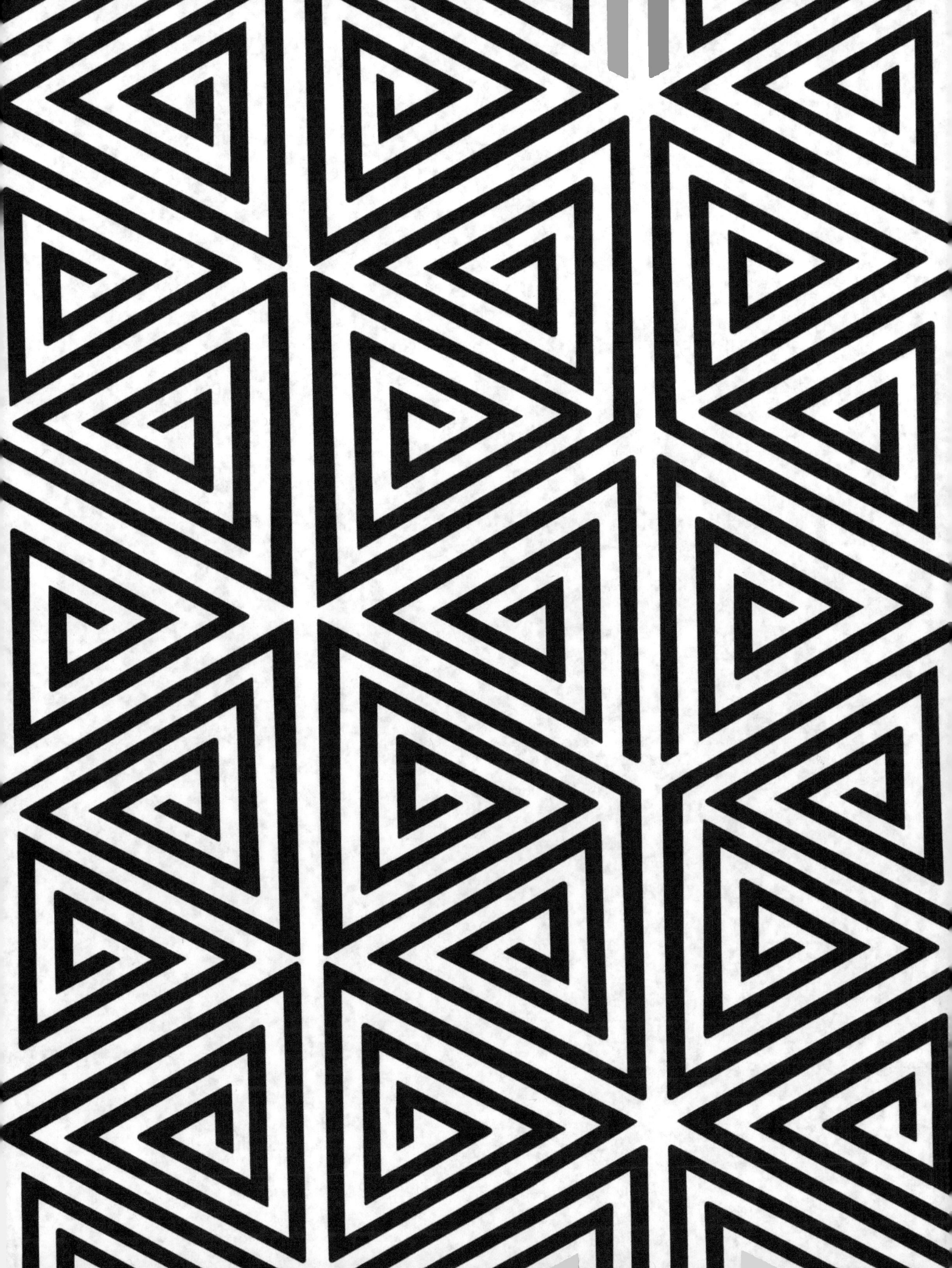

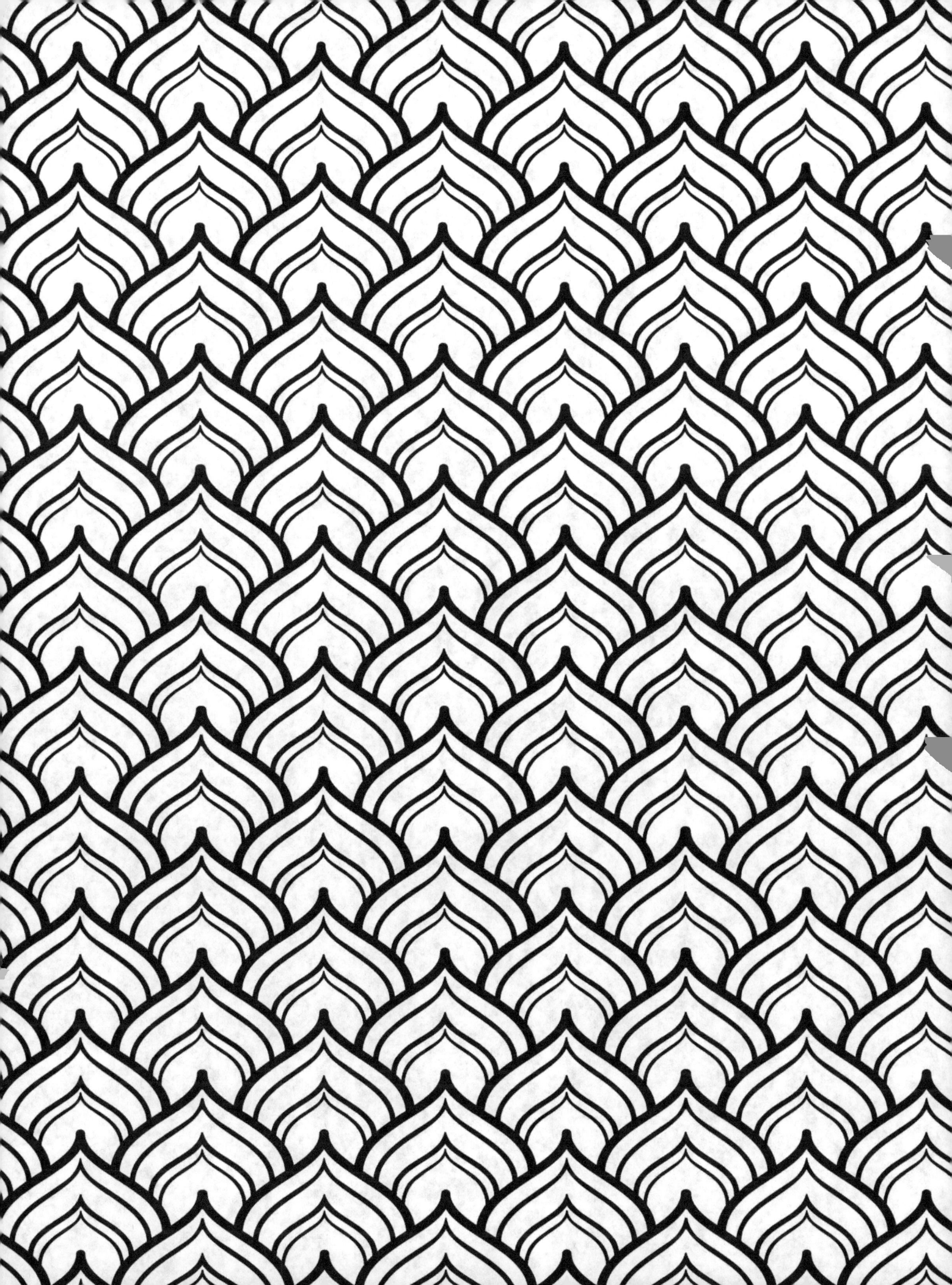

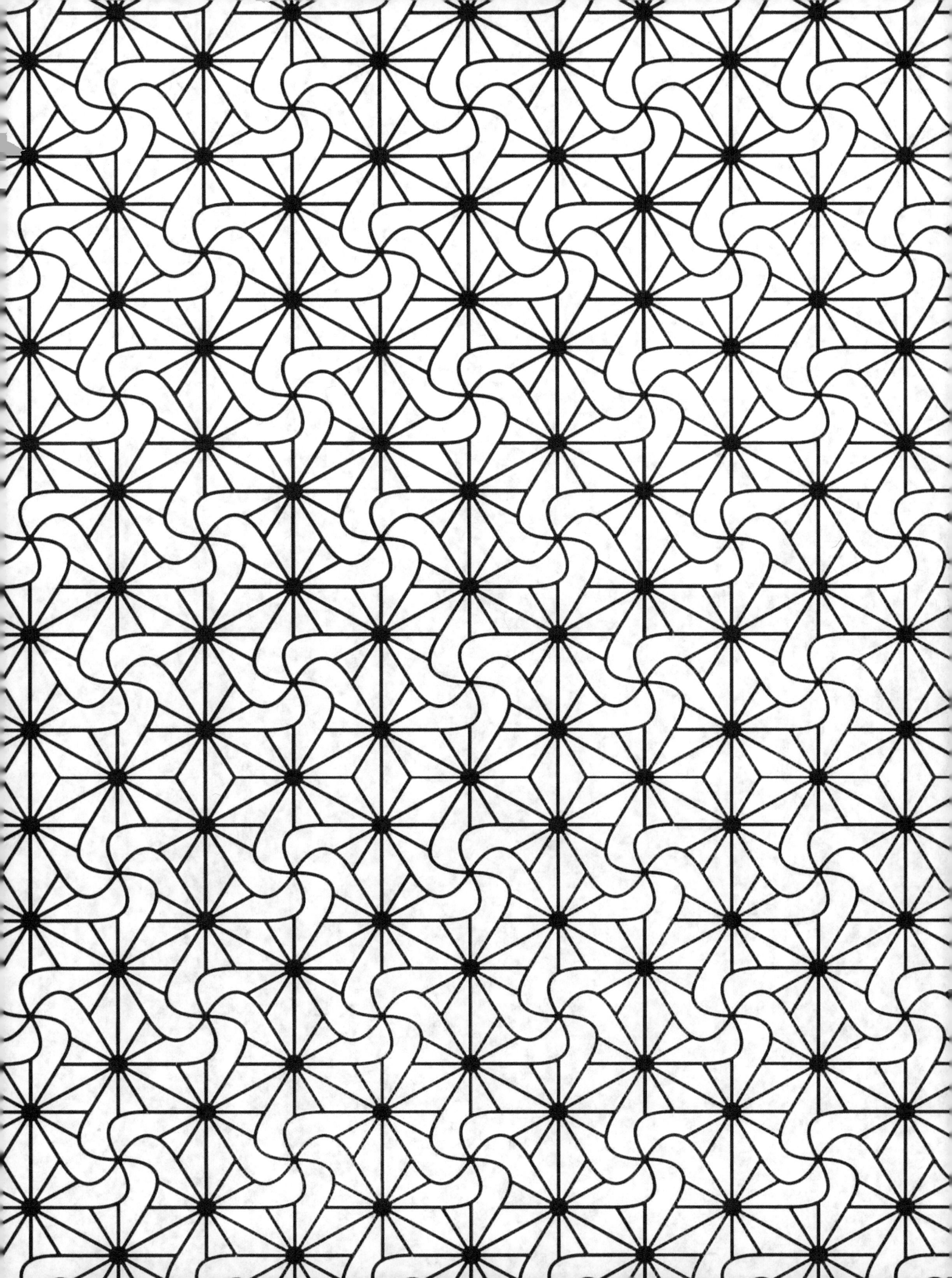

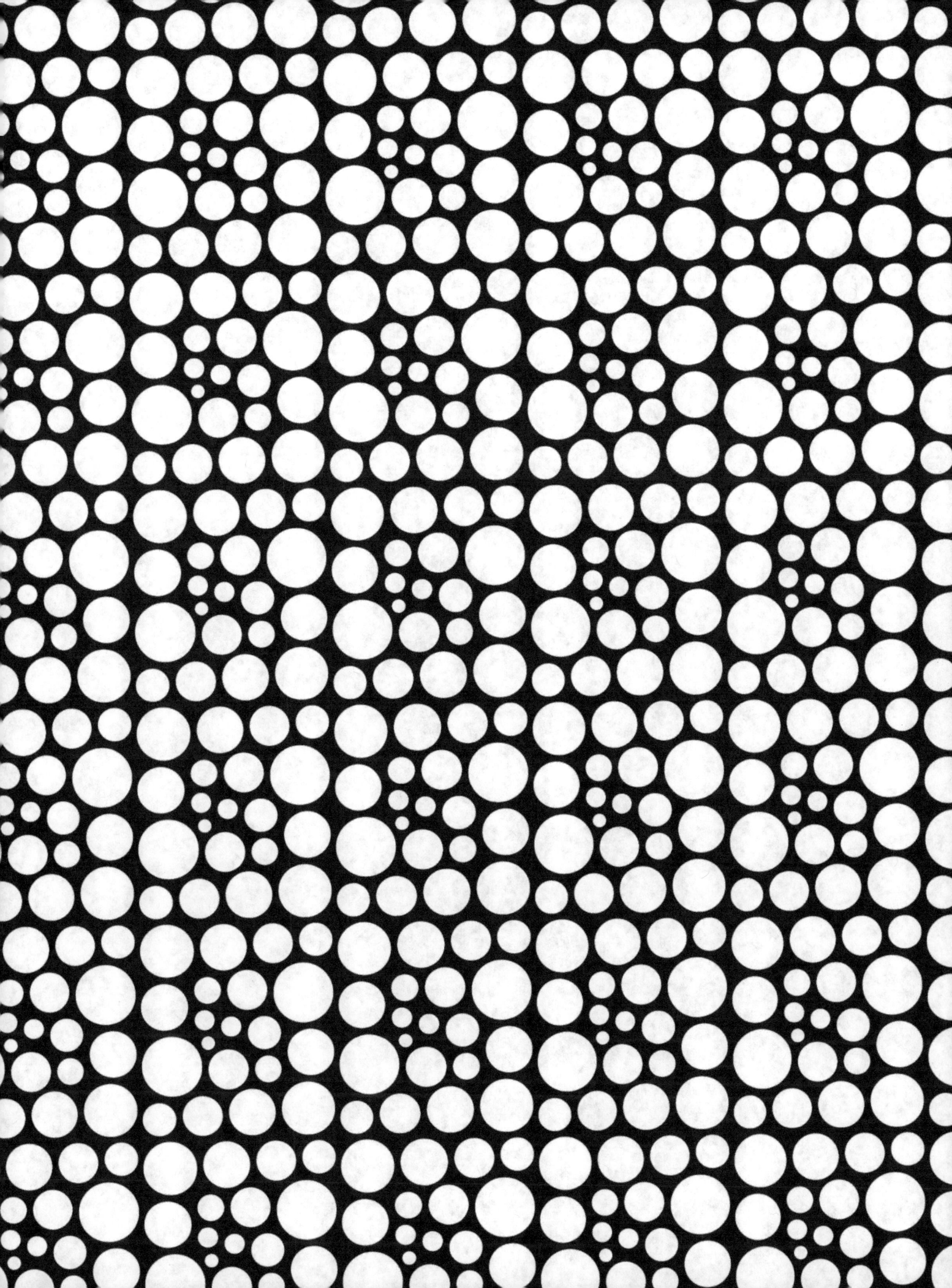

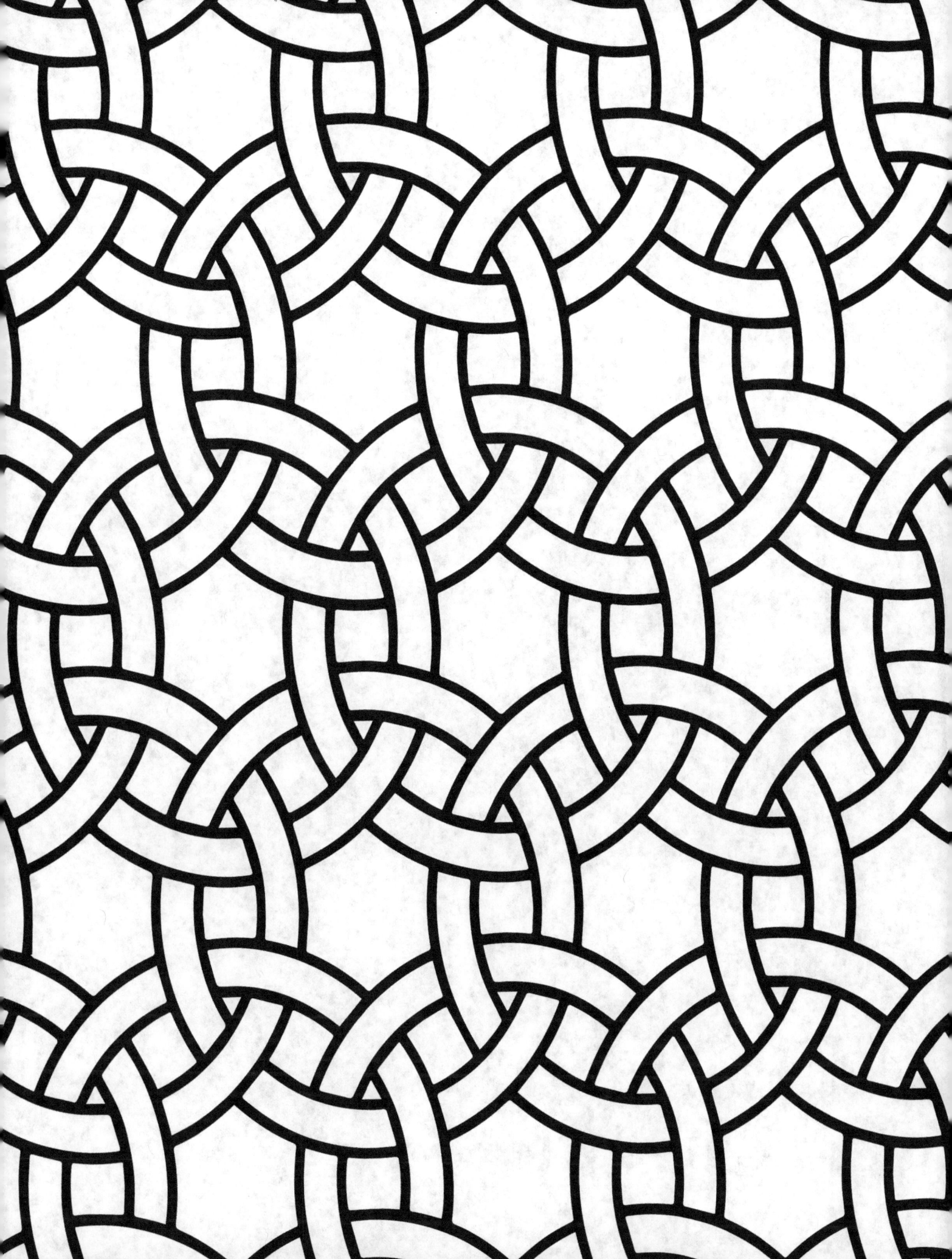

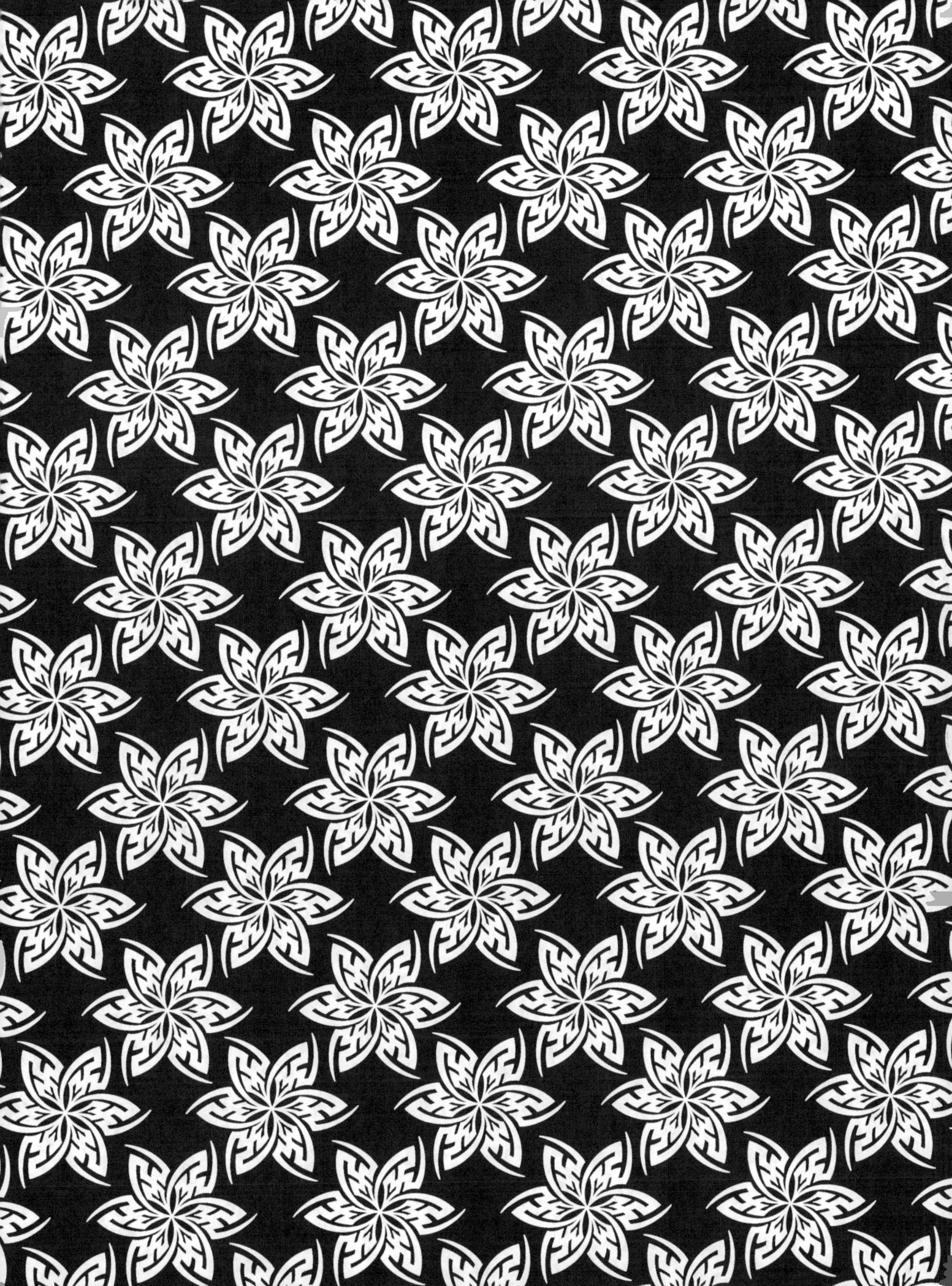

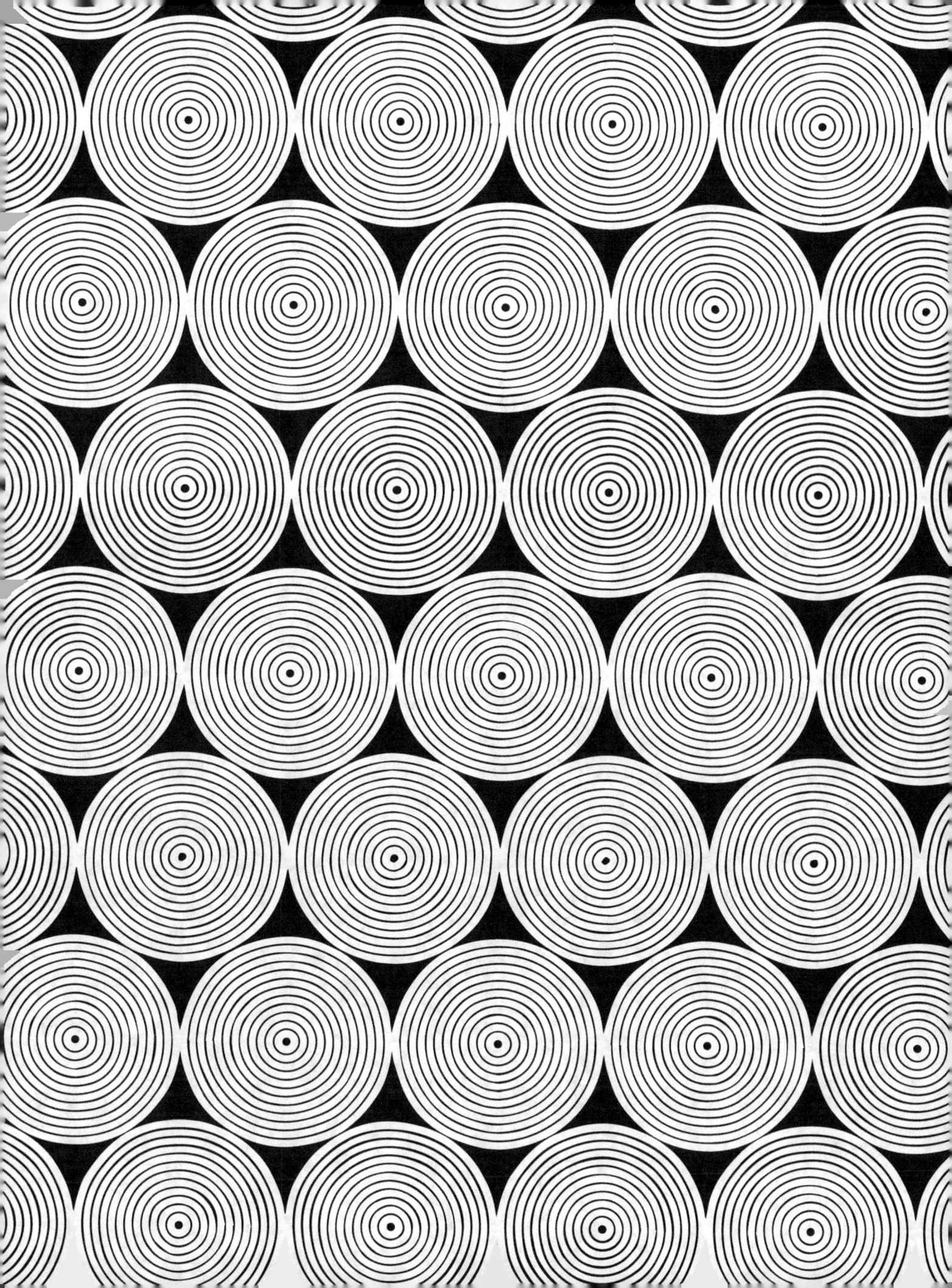

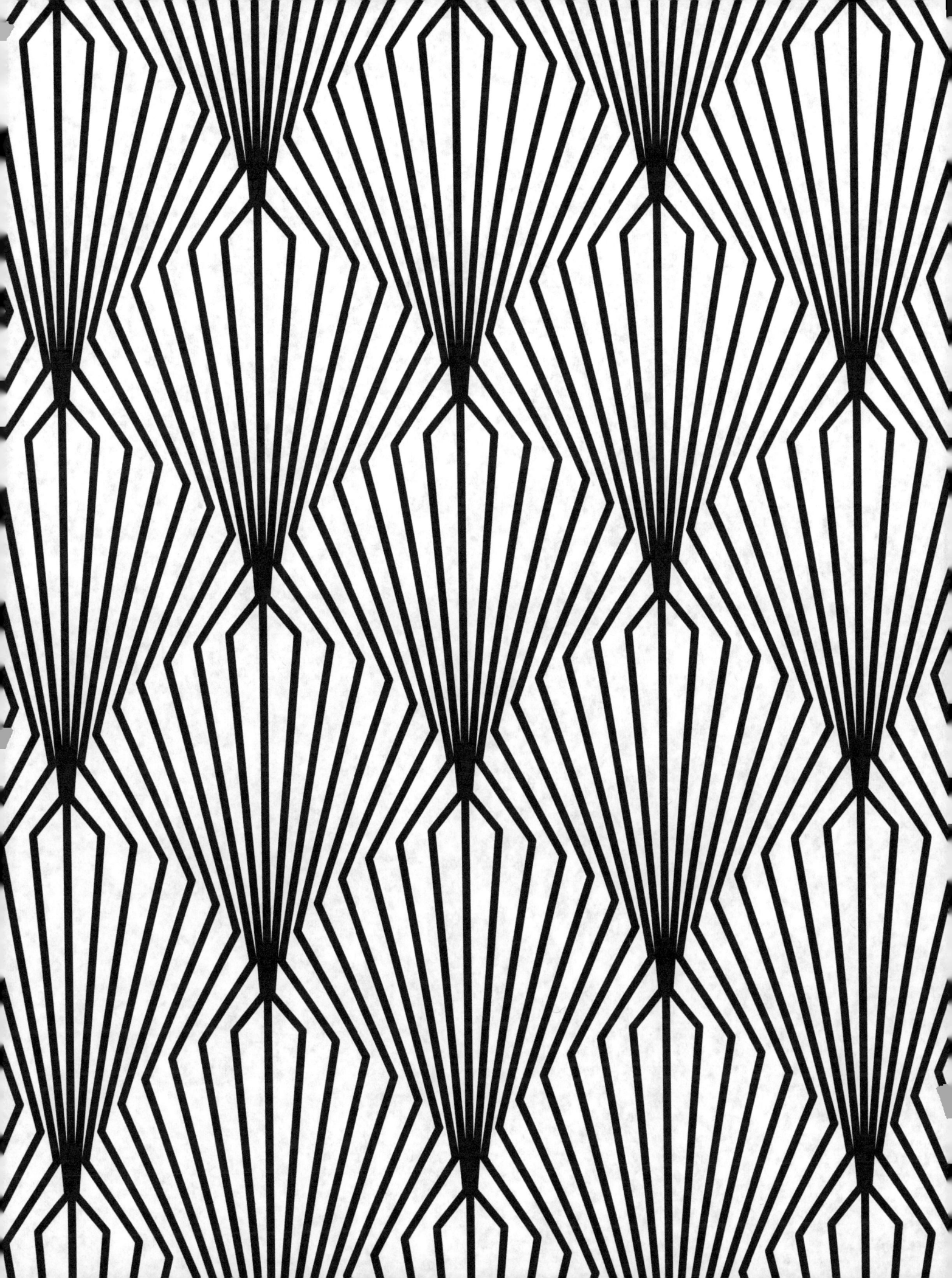

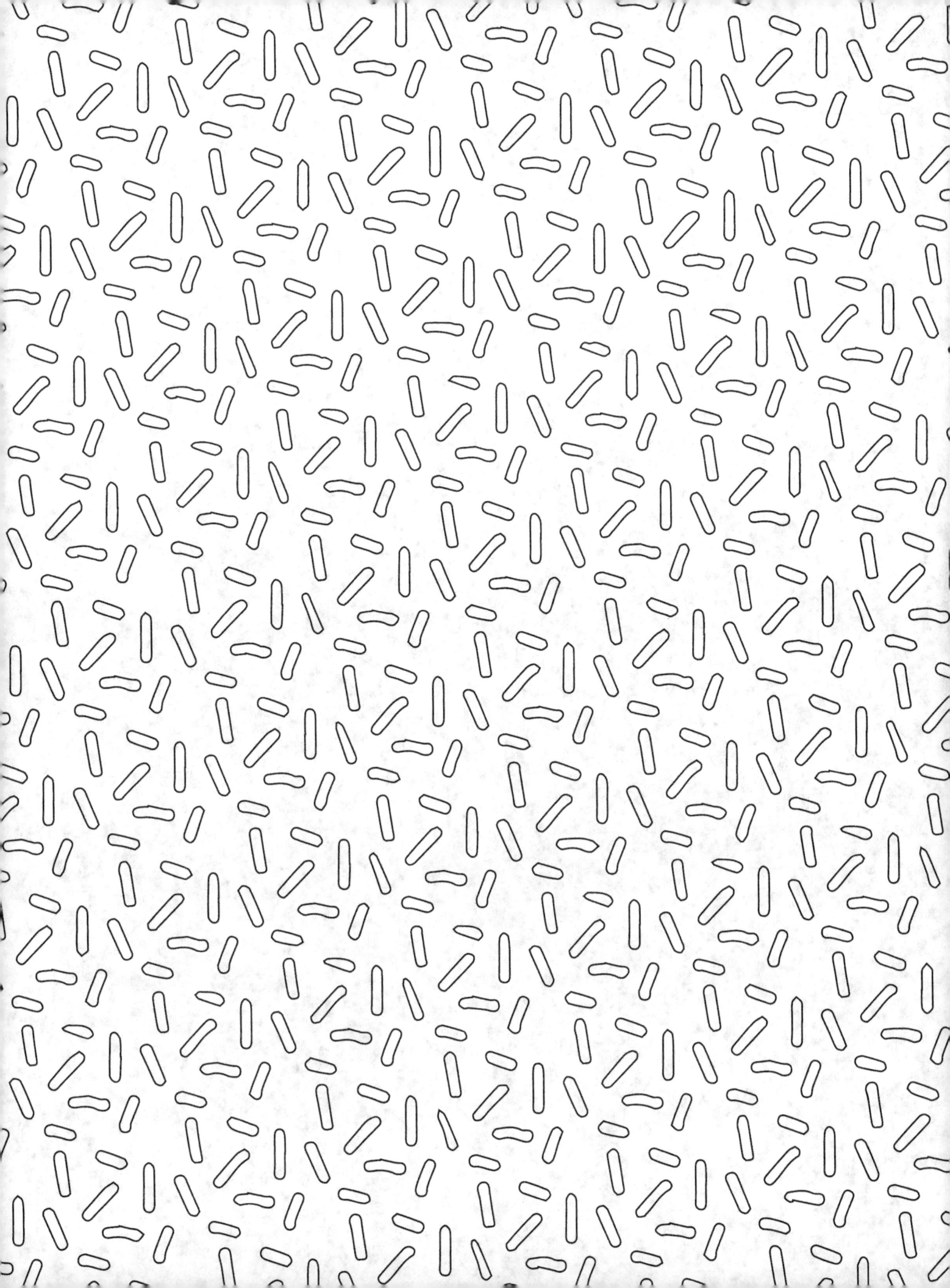

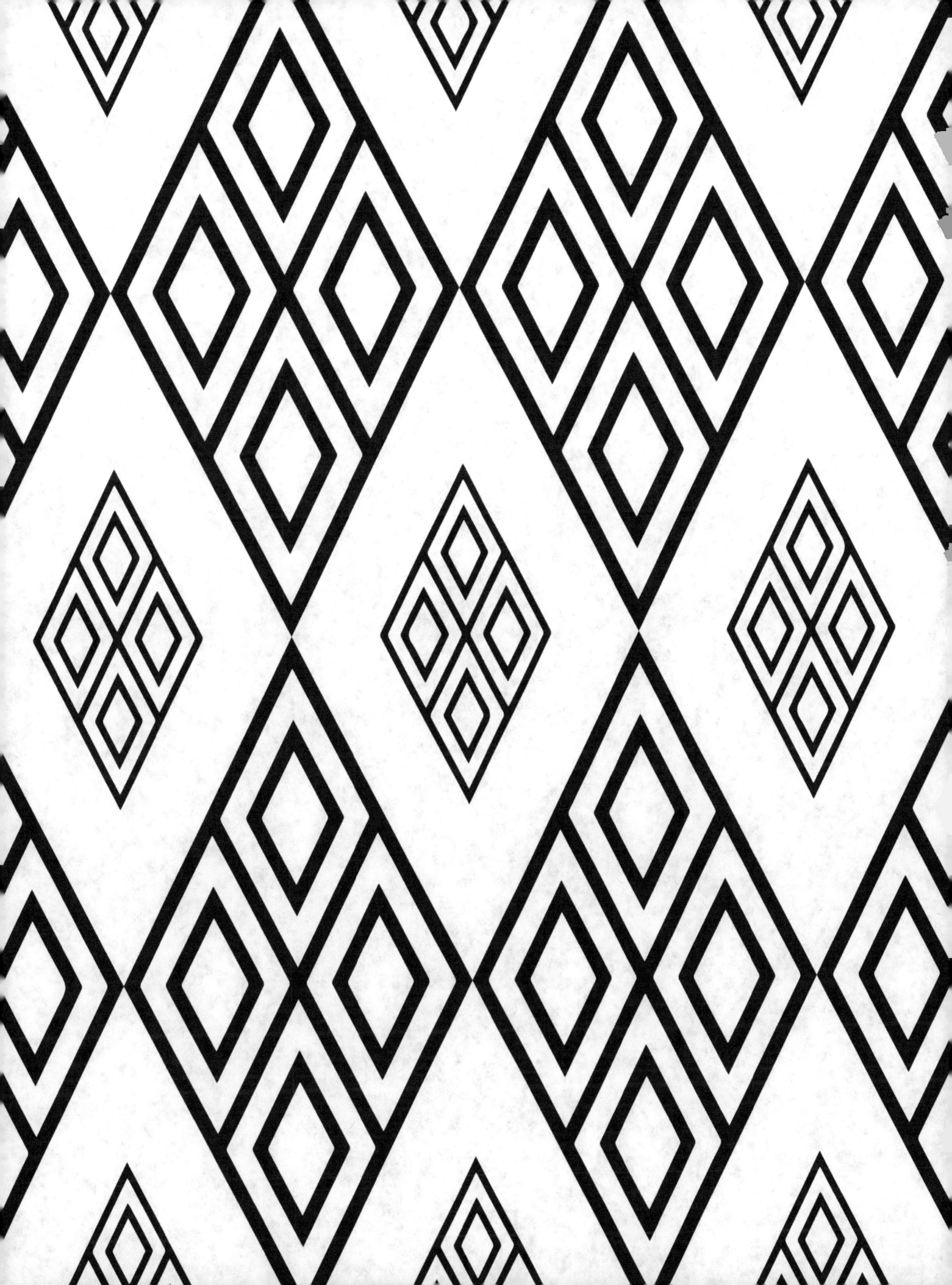

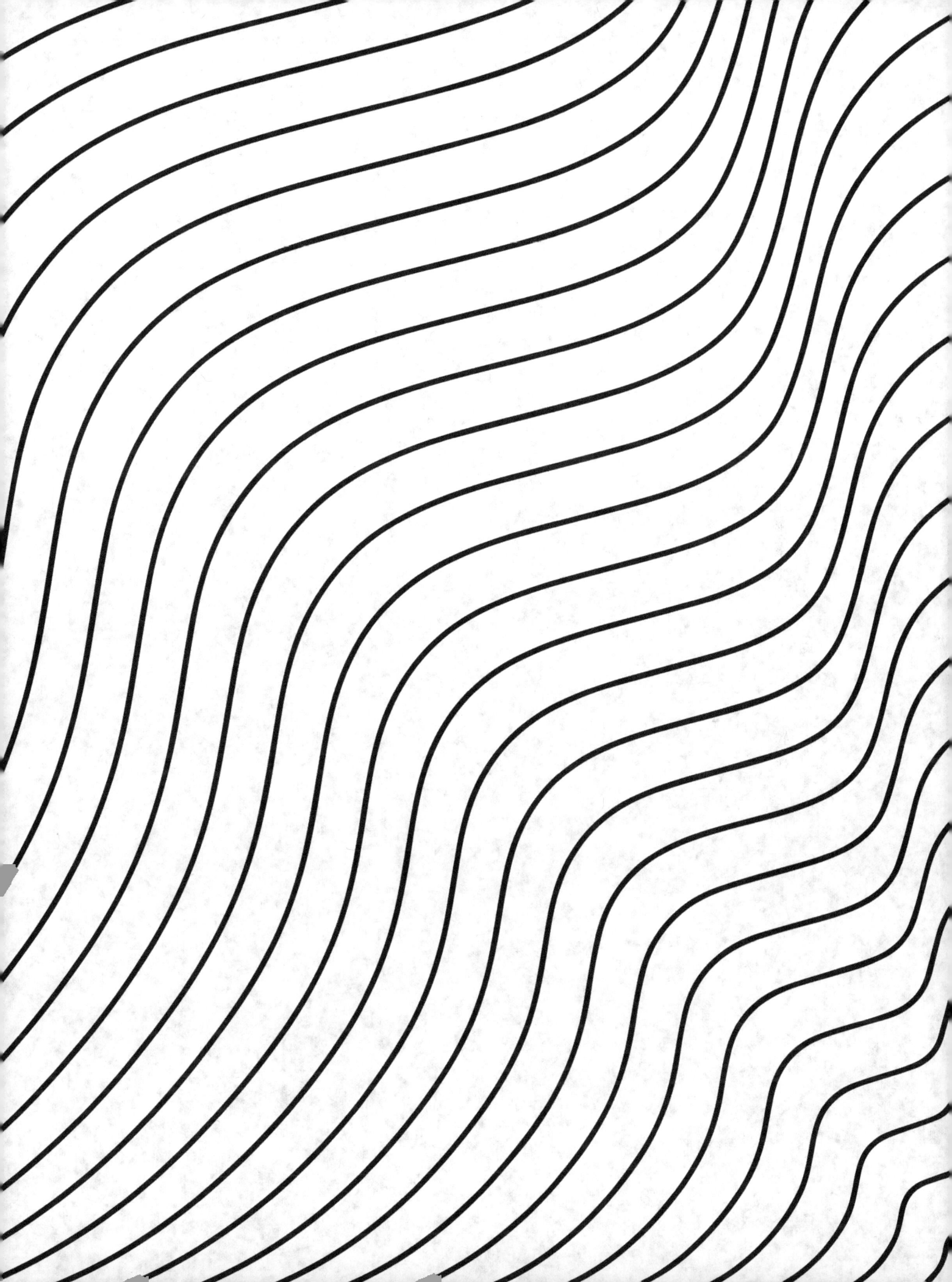

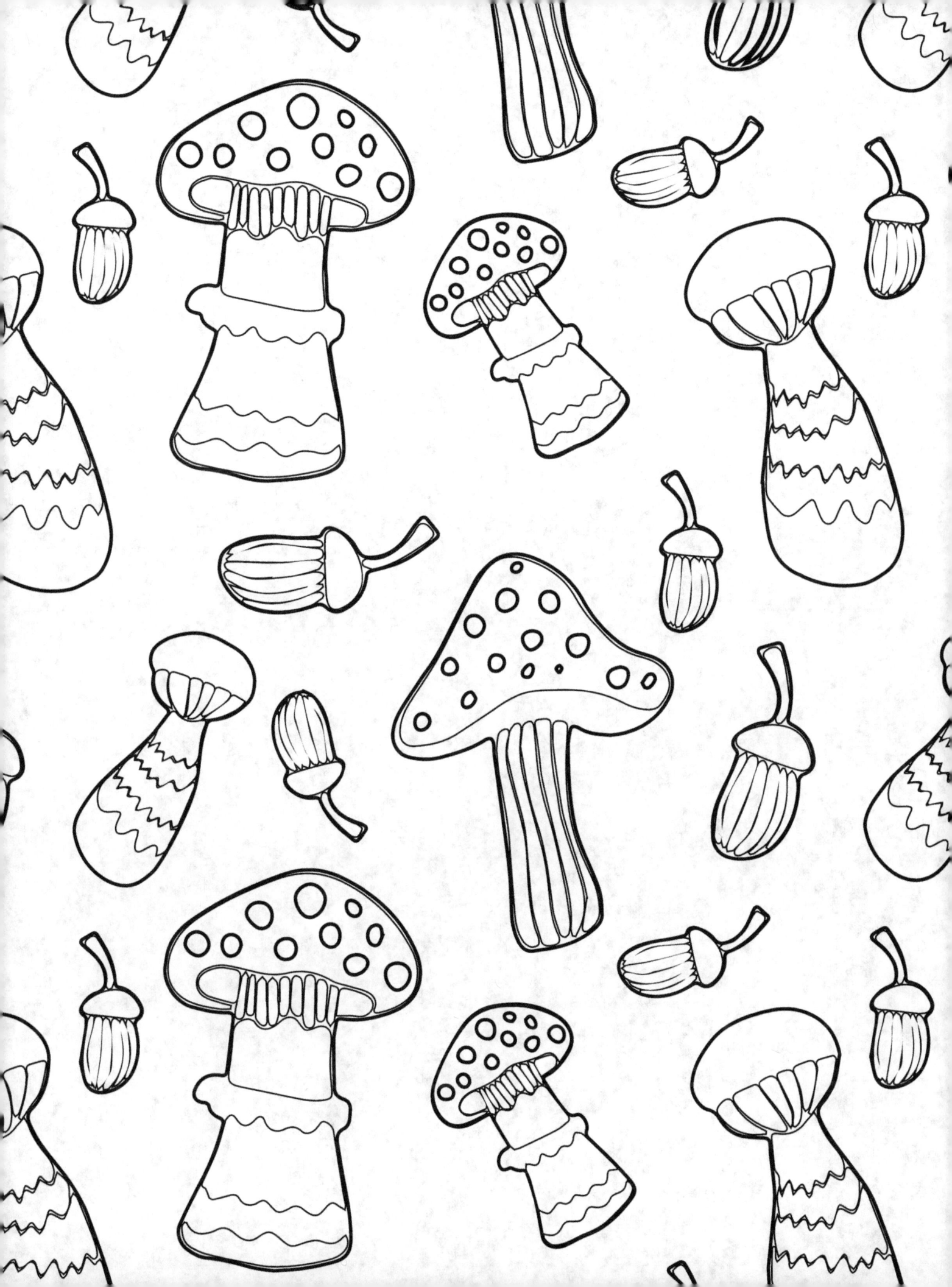

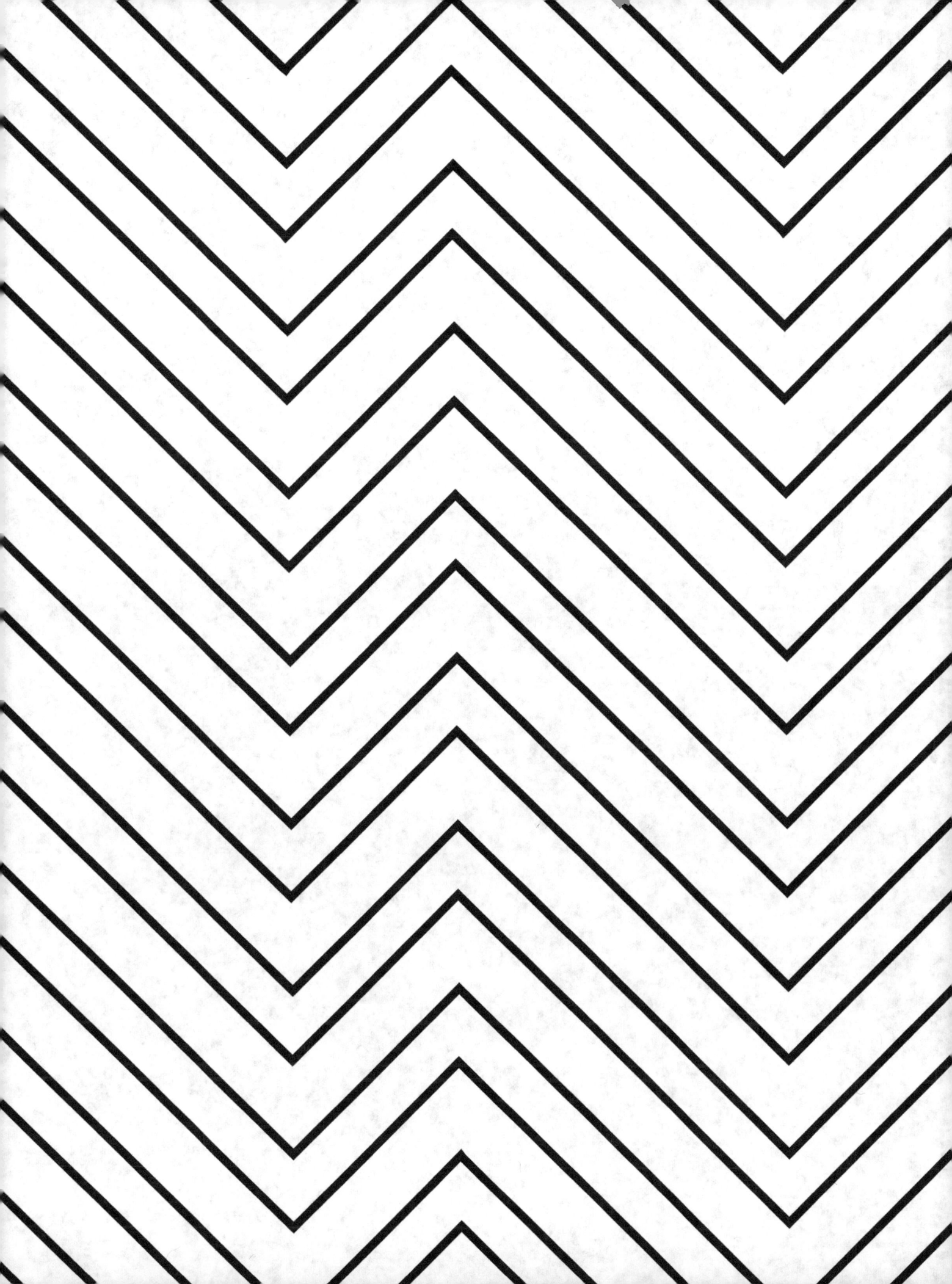

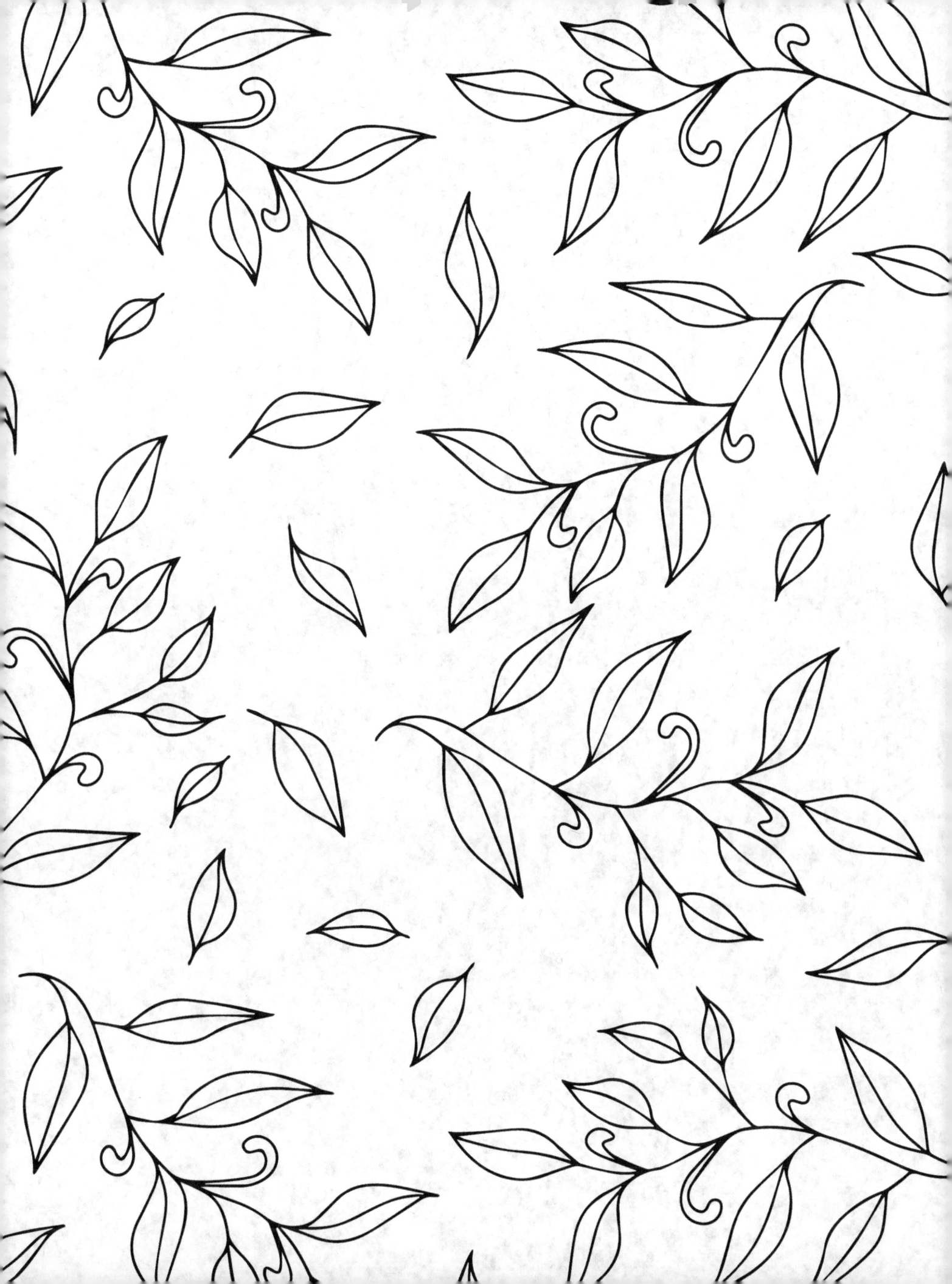

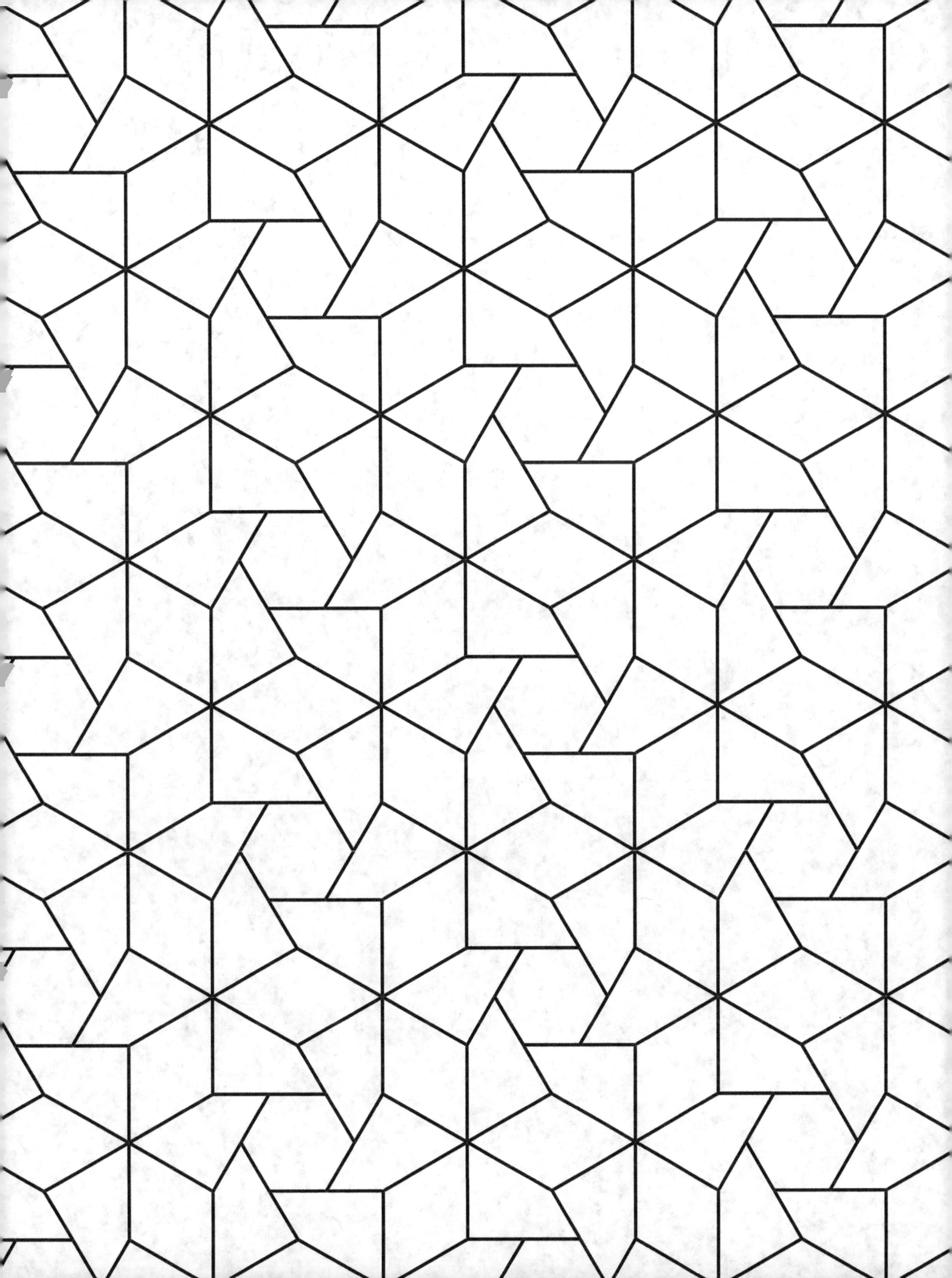

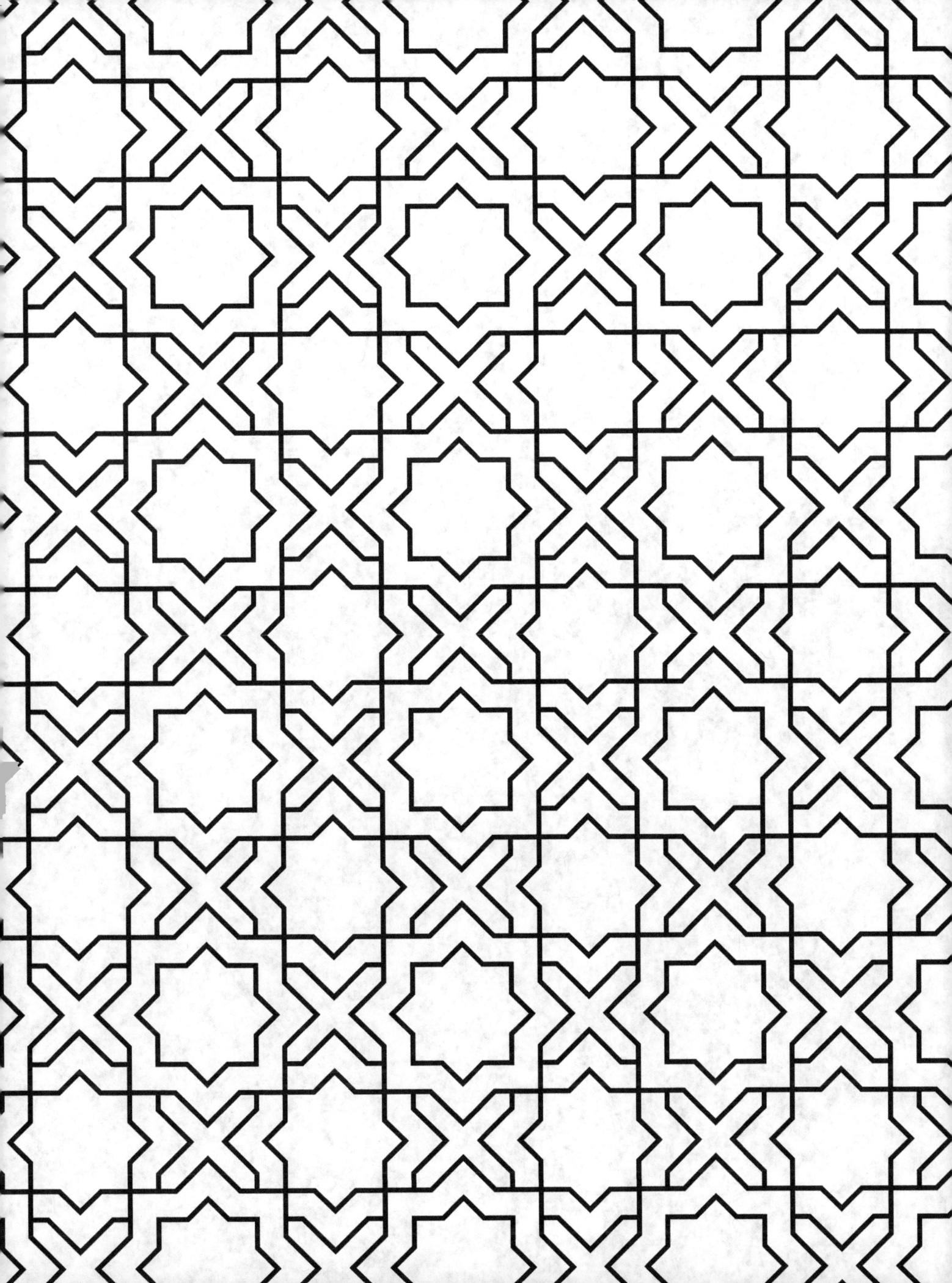

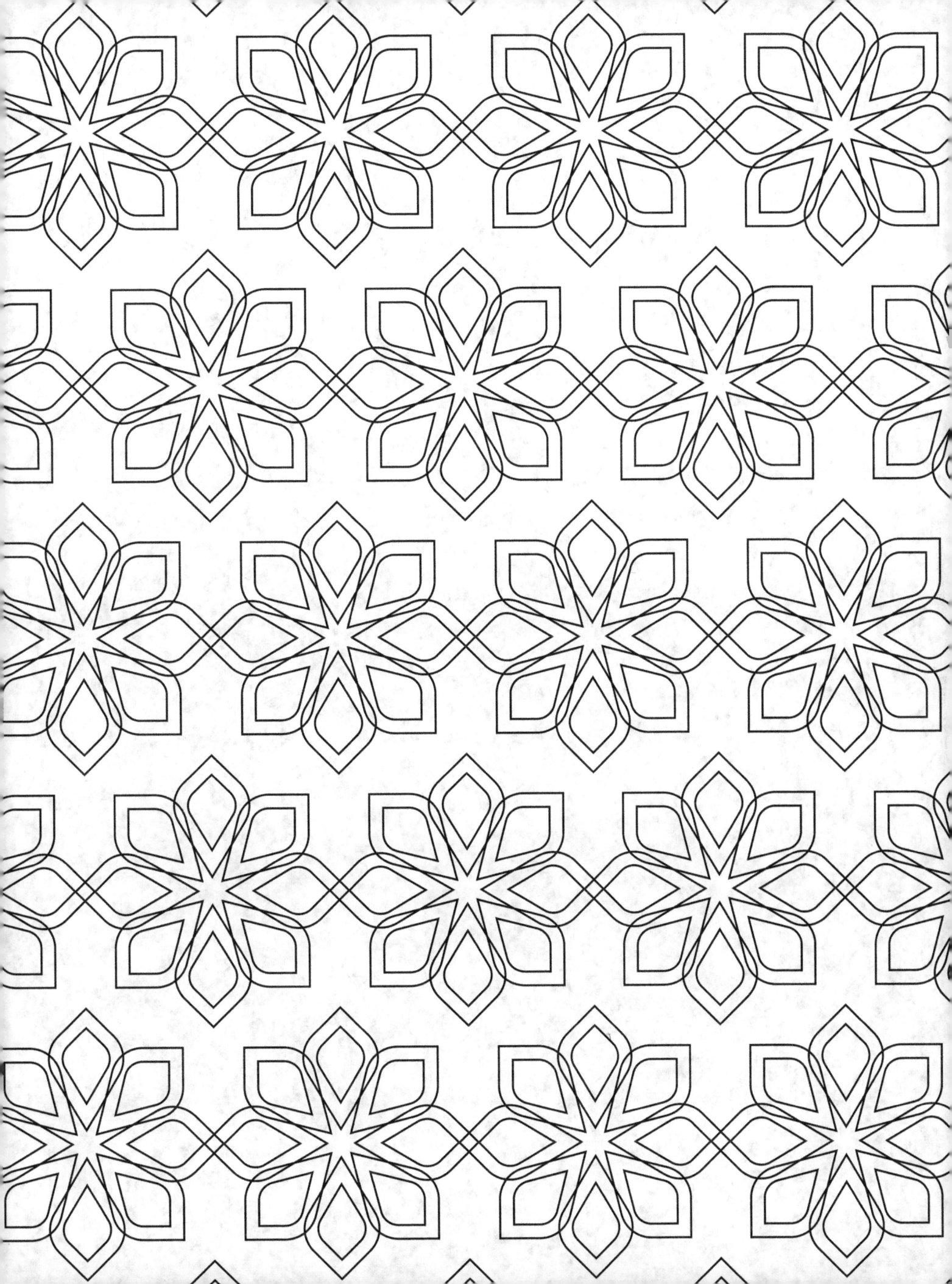

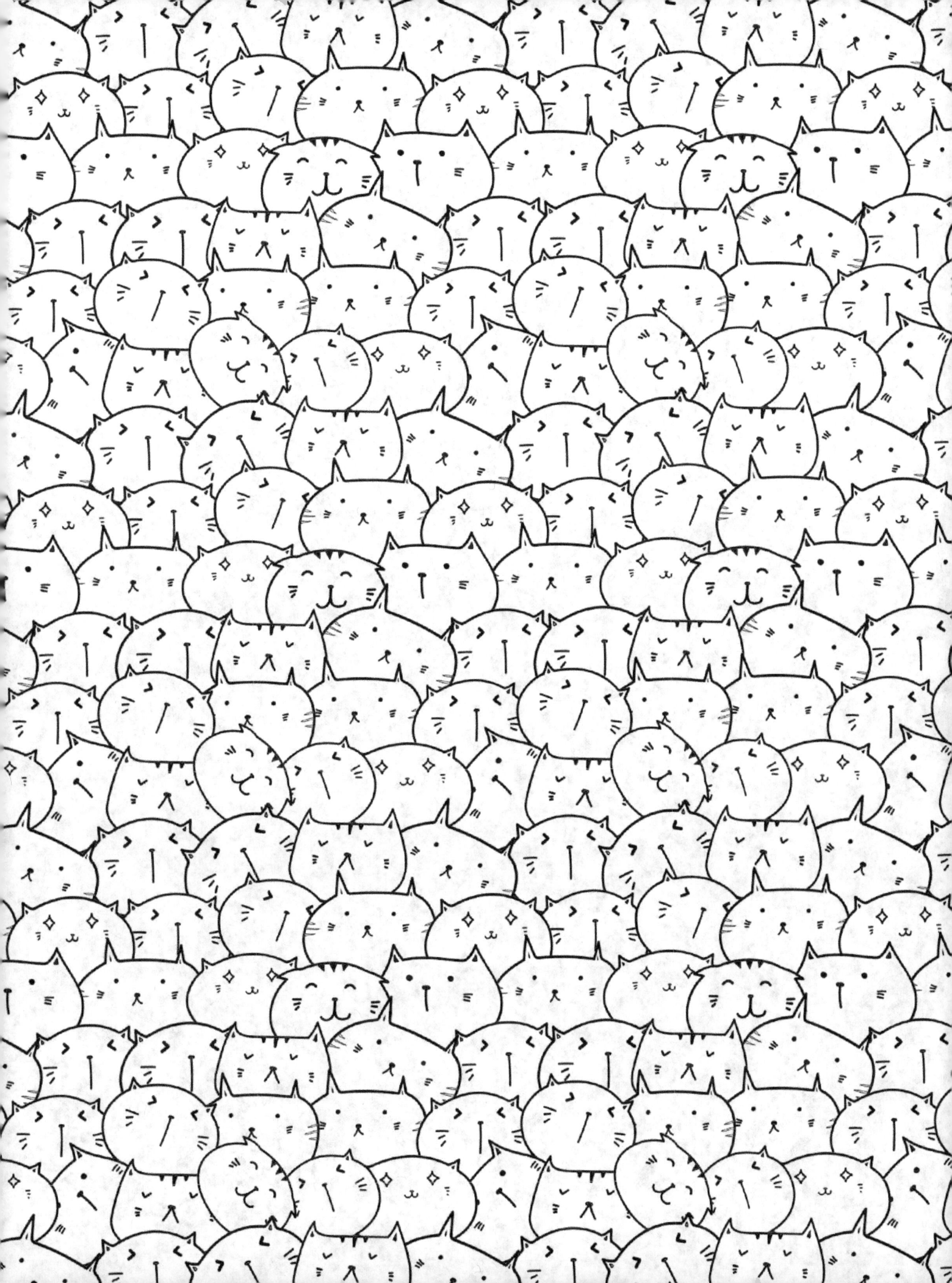

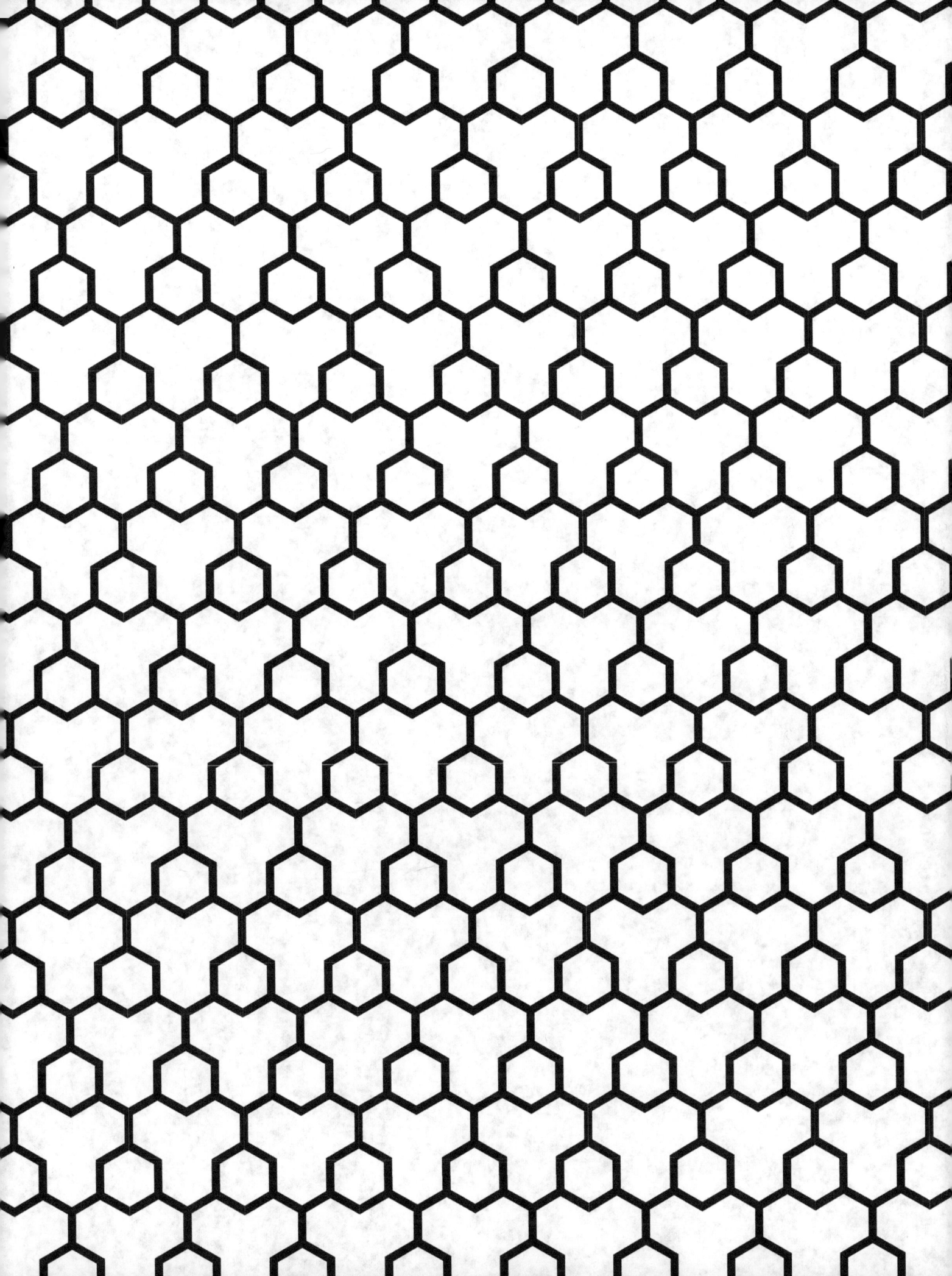

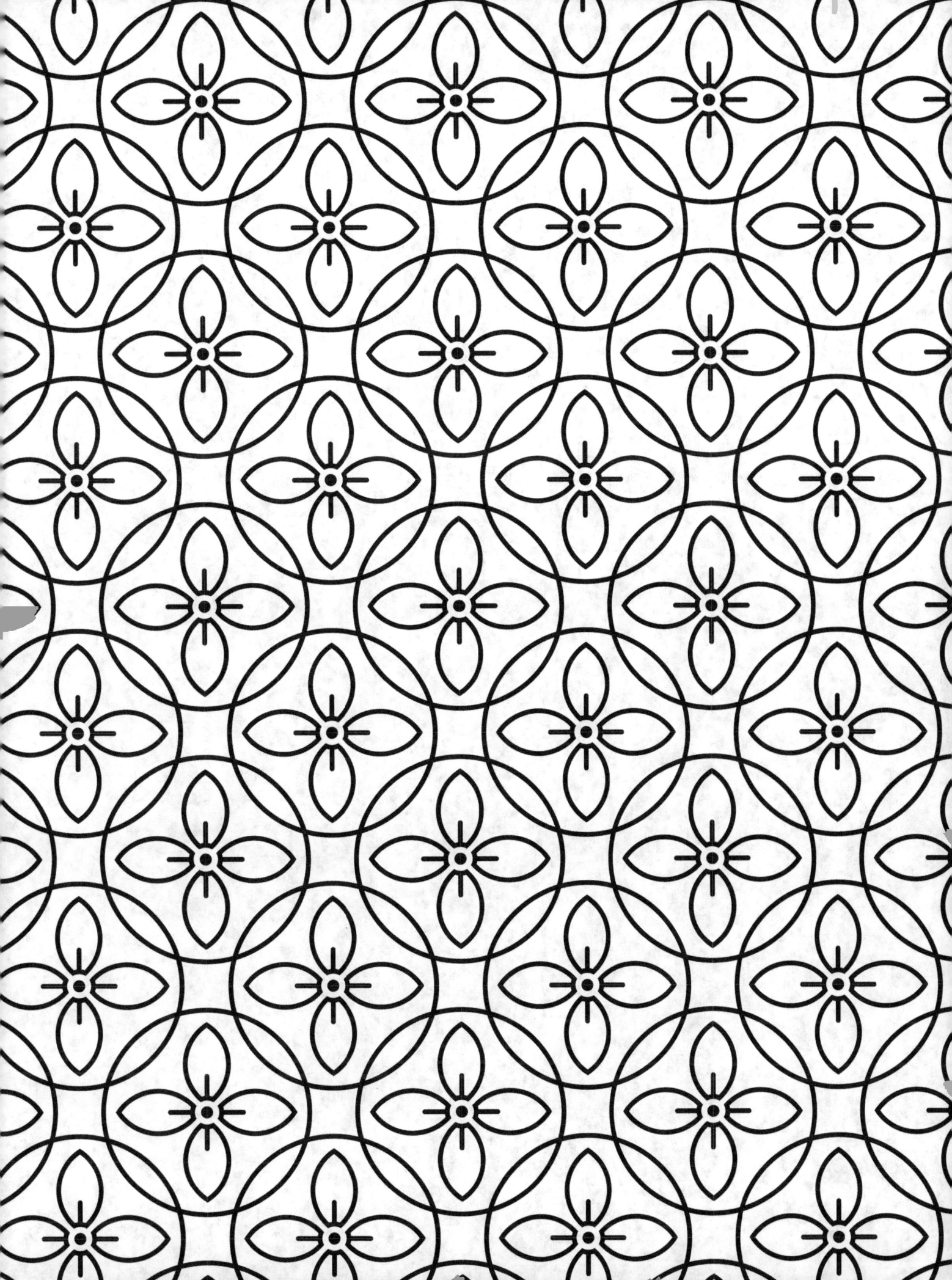

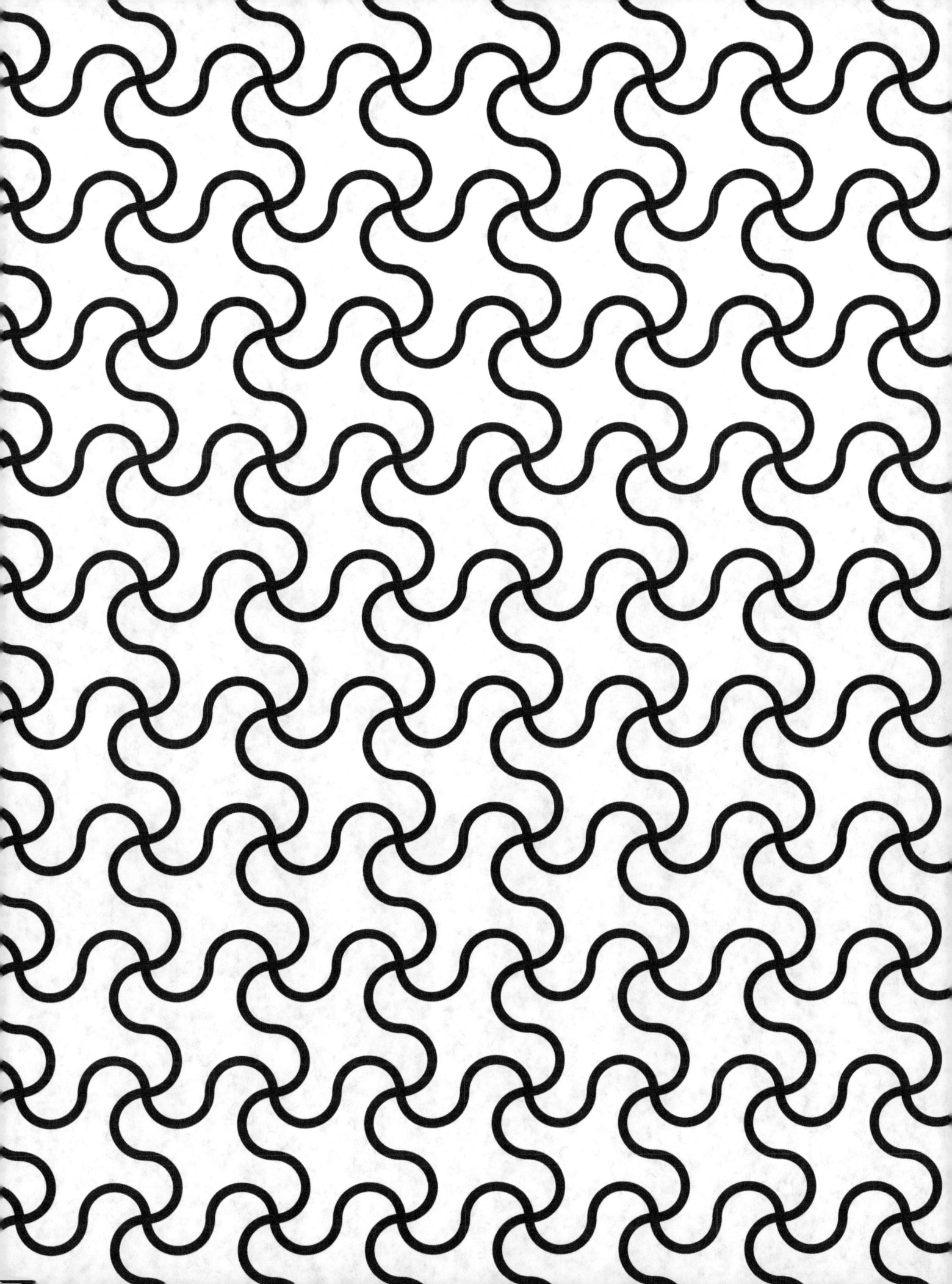

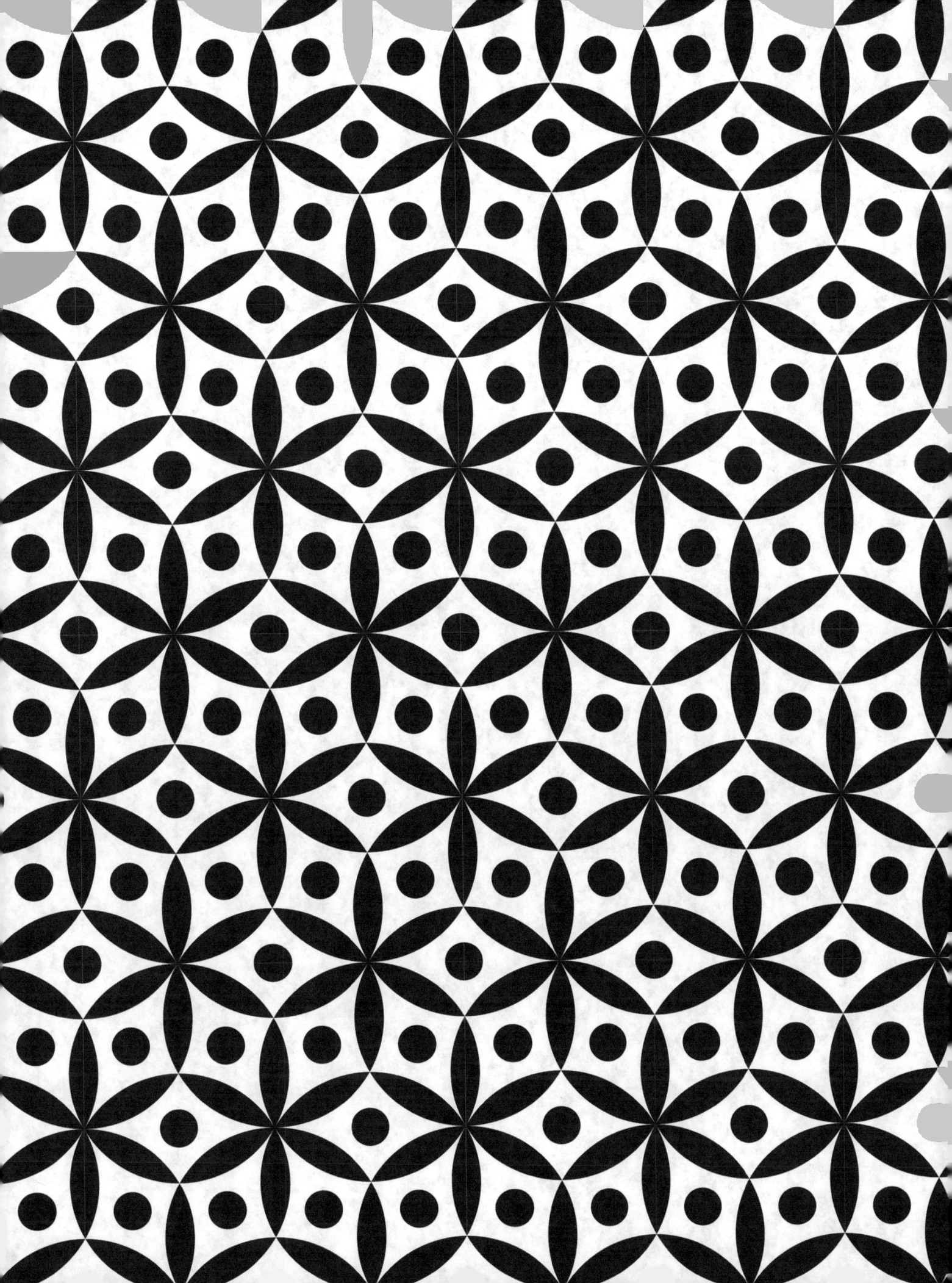

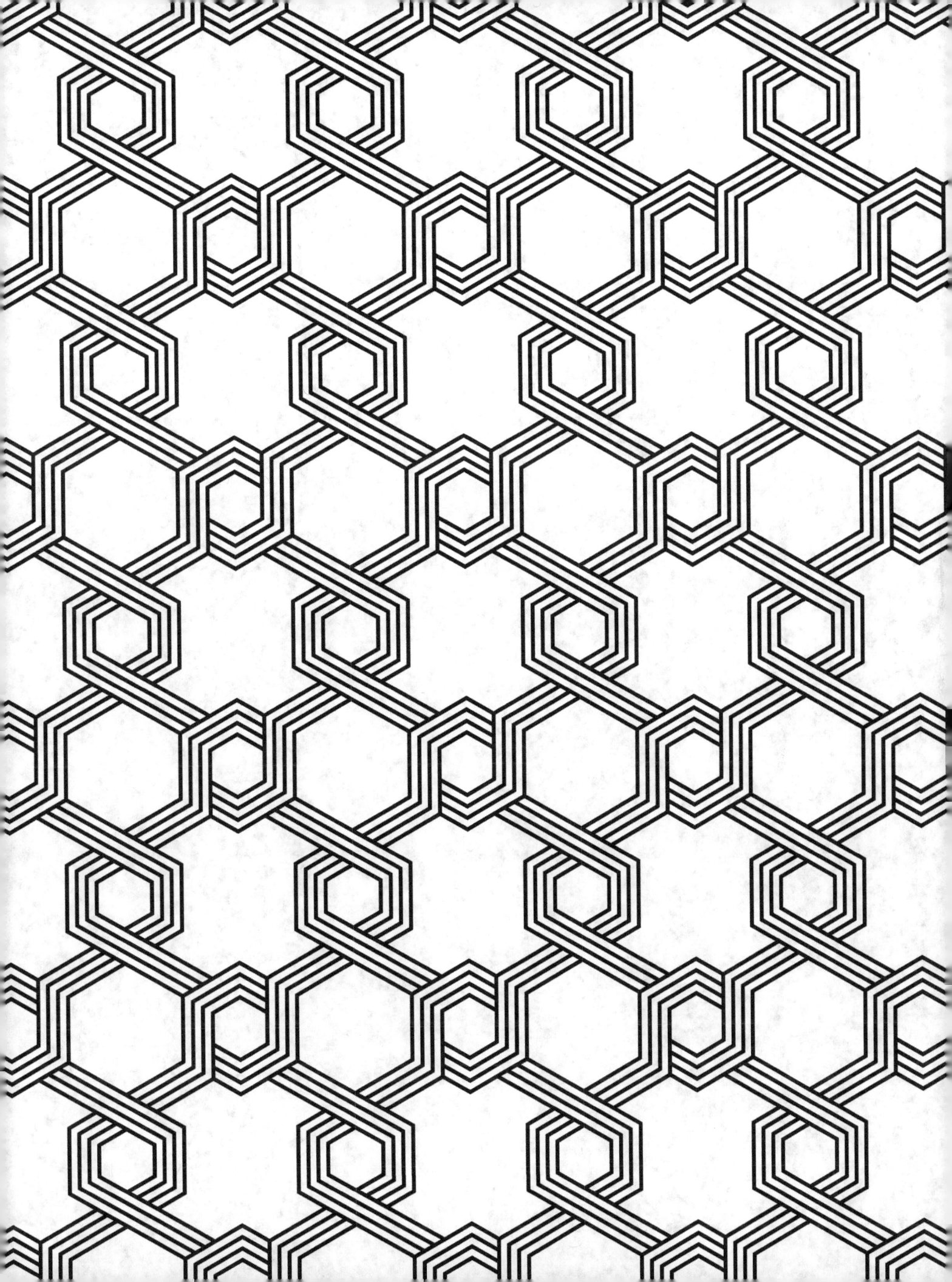

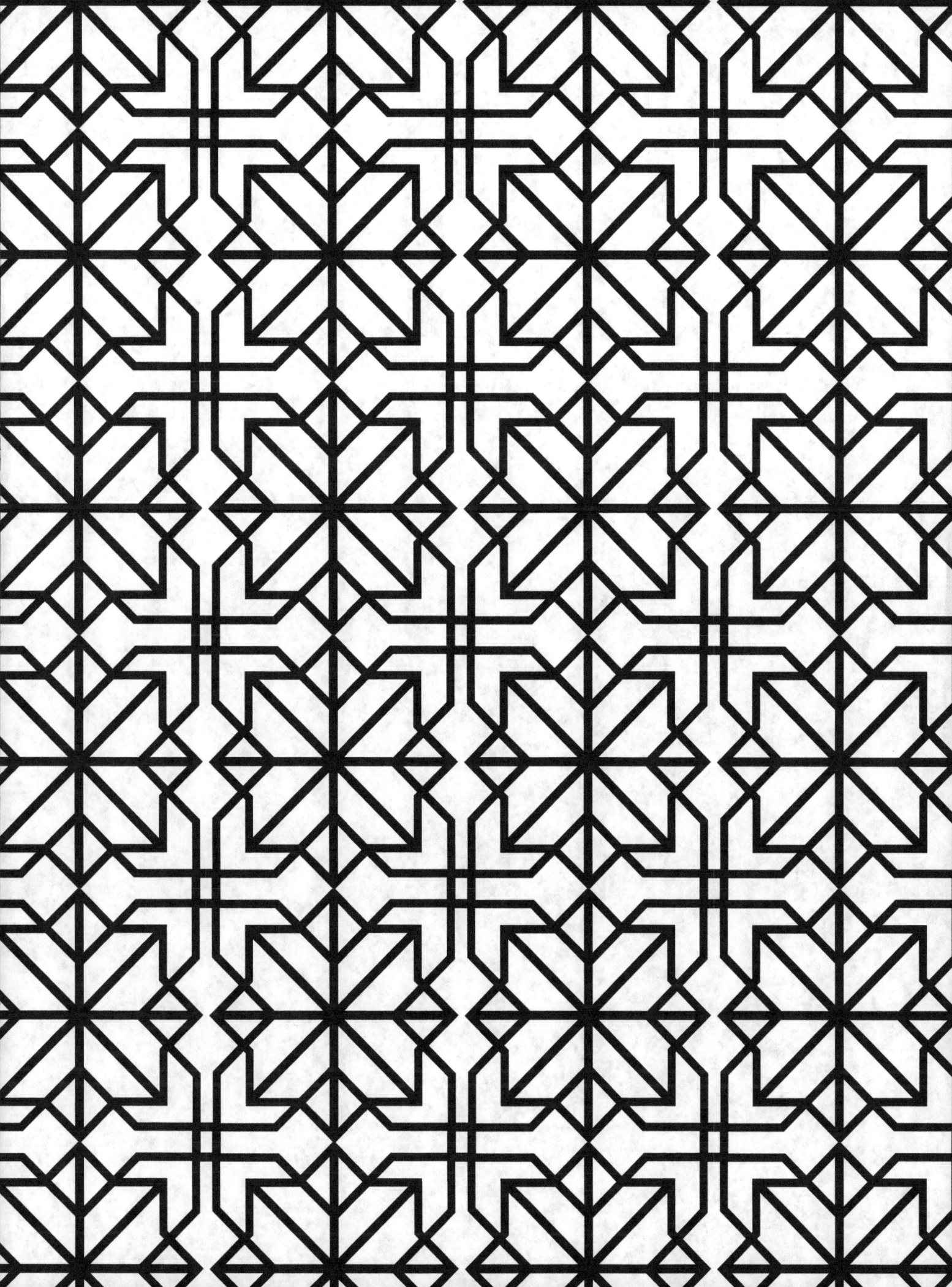

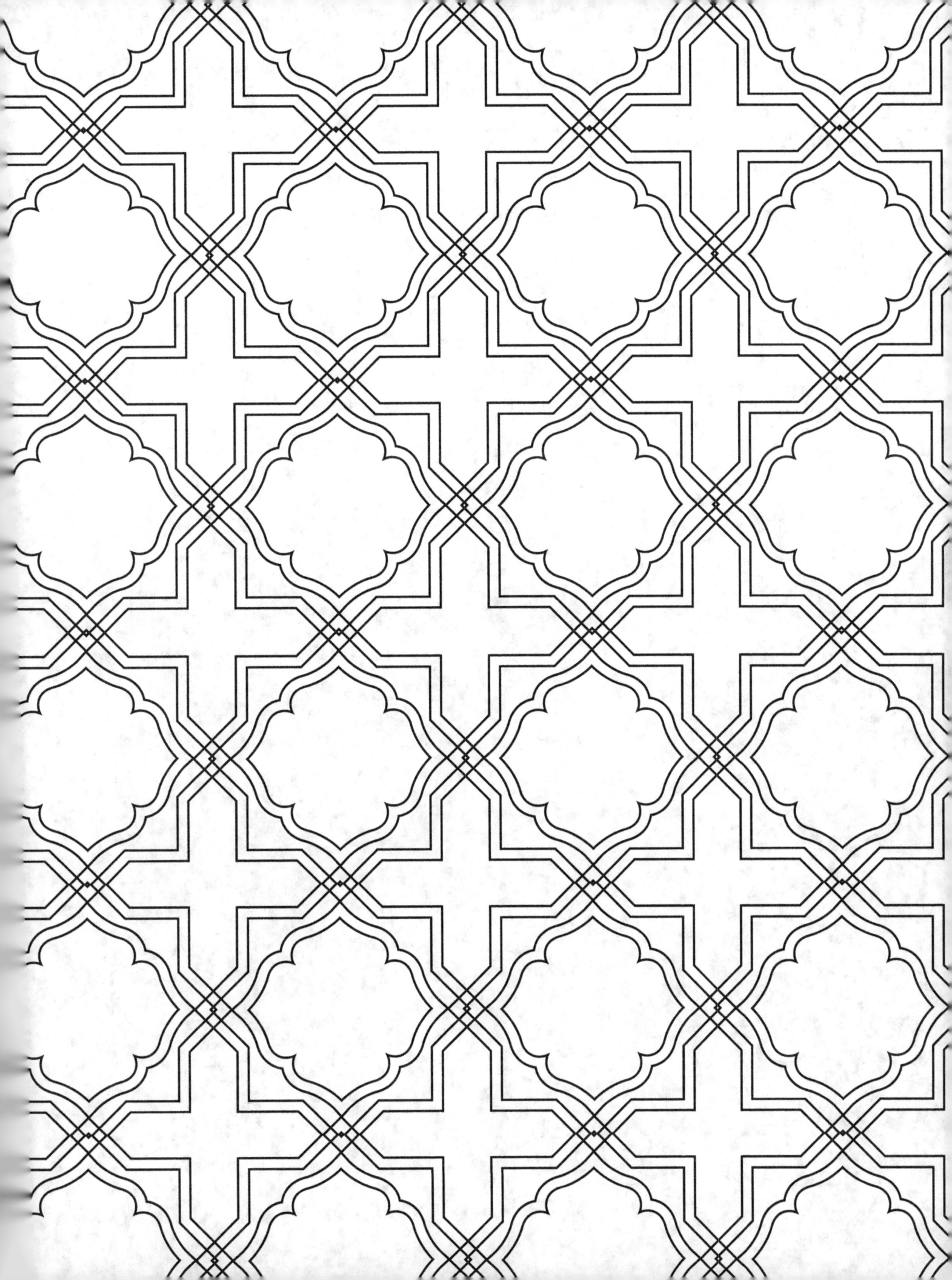

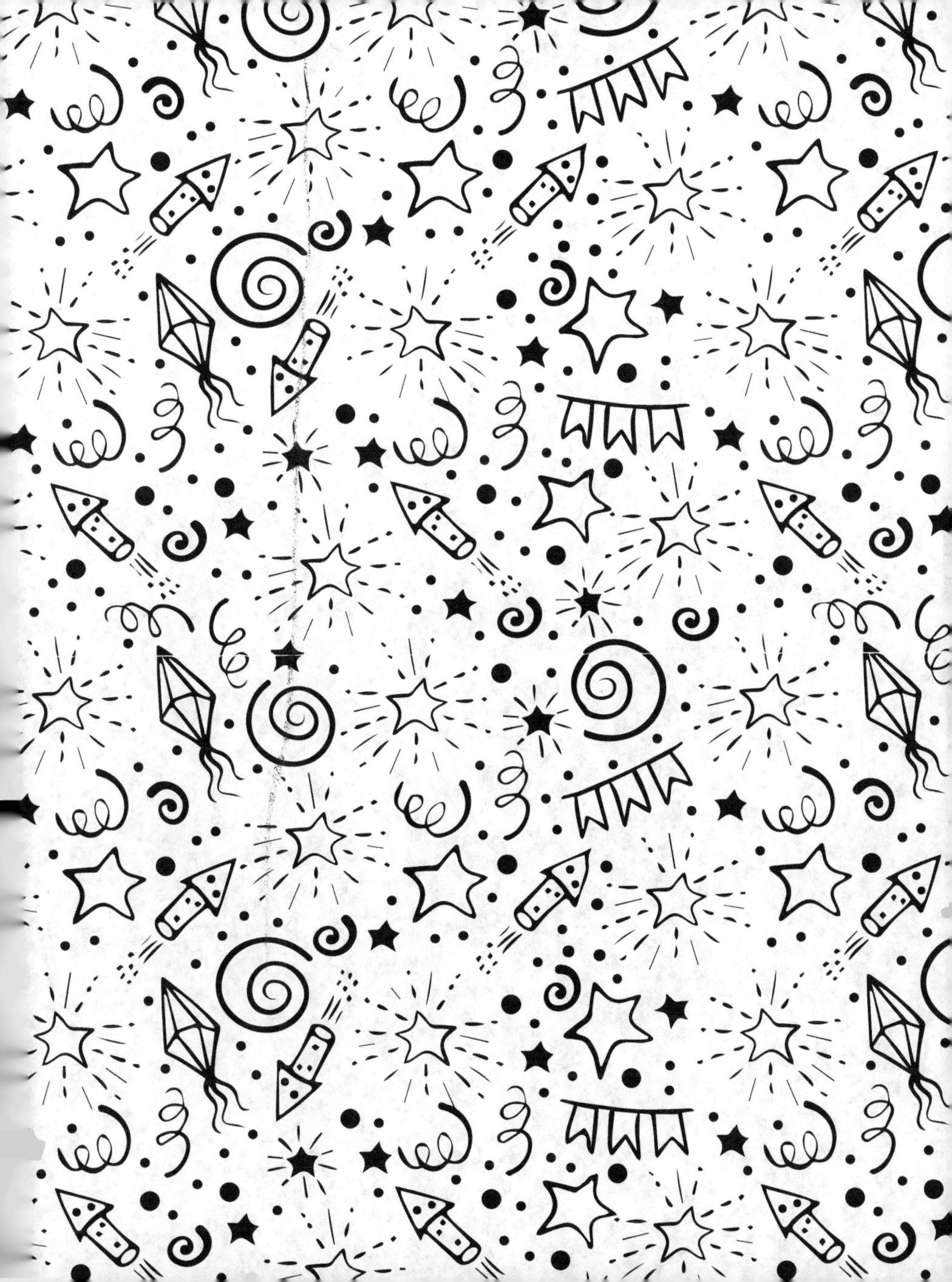

Bleeder Page #1

BLEED ON ME WHEN YOUR INK IS TOO STRONG

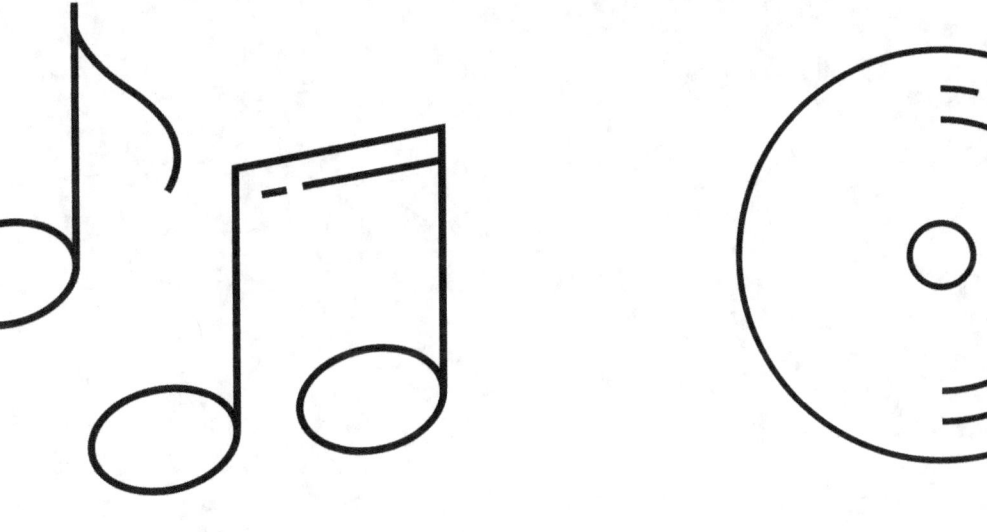

Bleeder Page #2

AND I'LL BE YOUR PEN. I'LL HELP YOU COLOR ON...

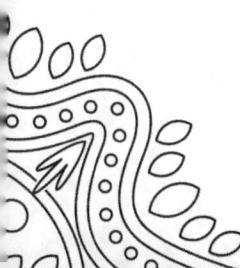
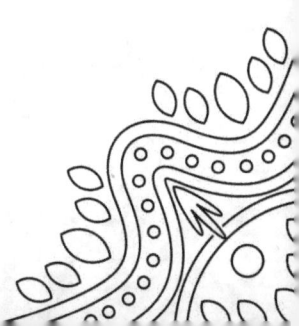

Bleeder Page #3

FOR IT WON'T BE LONG TIL YOU'RE GOING TO NEED

Bleeder Page #4

SOME PAPER TO BLEED ON

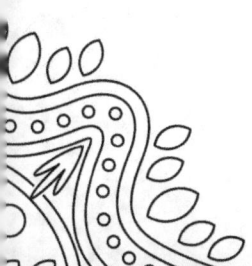
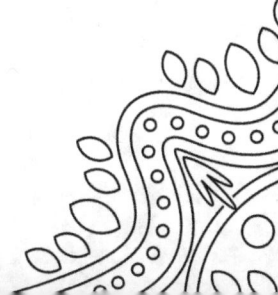

More Fun Coming Soon!

Give us a follow on Instagram for free coloring pages, contests, and news on upcoming coloring books!

@meghanjamescreations